More Praise for

REAL
TIME

"Regis McKenna's insights will excite you and shock you.
Best of all, they will get you thinking about how to survive in a future world
where things happen so quickly that every current
business interaction and process must be radically overhauled."
—LEW PLATT, Chairman and CEO, Hewlett-Packard

"The race is on for real time information in marketing. As in future military
engagements, the need for up-to-the-minute information is the key
to success. The rapid advances in communications and computer technologies
are outstripping our current managers' mind-set and ability to seize
the opportunities afforded to them. Regis McKenna explains how and why
we must open our thinking to take advantage of real time information."
—J. D. POWER III, Chairman and Founder, J. D. Power & Associates

"To succeed today, companies must learn how to
use information and telecommunications technology to respond
immediately, not only to changing circumstances but also
to customer demands. Regis McKenna's insightful book points out that
businesses can use intranets, extranets, and the Internet to create
dynamic information systems that accomplish both of these goals."
—JAMES L. BARKSDALE
President and CEO, Netscape Communications Corporation

"Regis McKenna has written an insightful and useful book that provides a
practical understanding of how time, technology, and customer
service are increasingly interrelated. FedEx was founded on the principle that
business processes can be improved by compressing time, and we believe
Mr. McKenna is correct in his assertions that the demand for new technologies
and customized service will only accelerate in the future global economy."
—FRED SMITH, Chairman and CEO, Federal Express

—more—

"Regis McKenna never ceases to challenge the
conventional wisdom. The notion of eliminating hierarchy and long-term
planning, and creating real time management that focuses on
delivery, results, and customer needs is a key revelation for companies
large and small. The use of networked technologies to enable the
creation of distributed, connected organizations has tremendous implications
for the next generation of competitiveness for industries of all types."
—JERRY YANG, founder, Yahoo!

"*Real Time* is both profound and prophetic, written by one of
the best qualified people in the industry who has both the historical as well
as the futurist perspective. *Real Time* focuses on three explosive ways
information technology will affect the near-term future: (1) our way of life,
both business and personal, will become real time, causing individuals
to think and act in real time; (2) real time systems will become a crucial part
of a unified business strategy, essential to obtaining and sustaining
competitive advantage; and (3) our world will continue on its rapid course
toward direct connectivity between individuals within common
communities of interest. The combination of these three factors will be
greater than $1 + 1 + 1 = 3$. It is more likely to equal 10+."
—TODD A. GARRETT, Senior Vice President, Chief Information Officer,
Procter & Gamble

"Regis McKenna's *Real Time* is the new theory of relativity for
marketing, managing, and living in today's world. From his visionary view
of our world that is changing in real time, McKenna gives
new meaning to the concepts of just-in-time and mass customization for
leadership and consumer communications."
—BILL FIELDS, former Chairman and CEO, Blockbuster Entertainment,
a Viacom Company

"This timely and crisp assessment of the digital revolution
shows business leaders how the revolution affects buyers' behavior and
ordinary business practices, where the never satisfied customer
will take us in the future, and—most important—why it matters."
—ISAO OKAWA, Chairman, Sega Enterprises, Inc.

REAL TIME

Regis McKenna

REAL TIME

PREPARING FOR THE AGE OF THE NEVER SATISFIED CUSTOMER

Harvard Business School Press
Boston, Massachusetts

Published by the Harvard Business School Press in hardcover, 1997;
in paperback, 1999

Copyright © 1997 by Regis McKenna

Printed in the United States of America

03 02 01 00 99   5 4 3 2   (pbk)

Photo credits: p. 48—Printed with permission from Hershey Foods Corporation;
p. 49—Reproduced with permission of PepsiCo, Inc. 1997, Purchase, New York.

Library of Congress Cataloging-in-Publication Data

McKenna, Regis.
     Real time: preparing for the age of the never satisfied customer /
Regis McKenna.
          p. cm.
     Includes bibliographical references and index.
     ISBN 0-87584-794-3 (hc)
     ISBN 0-87584-934-2 (pbk)
     1. Real-time data processing. 2. Technology—Sociological aspects.
I. Title.
HF5548.M365 1997
658.4'06—dc21
                                                                97-12475
                                                                     CIP

*The paper used in this publication meets the requirements of the American National
Standard for Permanence of Paper for Printed Library Materials Z39.49-1984.*

To Madeline, Conor, Molly, Bridget, and Brendan,
our grandchildren, for whom real time will be
real time

Contents

ACKNOWLEDGMENTS

I HAVE BEEN MOST FORTUNATE to live and work in Silicon Valley, around and with so many talented people, and to have access to the new tools of information and communications. *Real Time* is my fourth book. My first was published in 1986 and written, like the other two, on an Apple Macintosh. This book, however, is truly a child of networking and the Internet. My writer and editor and longtime friend, Cheryll Barron, lives 400 miles from San Francisco, somewhere near the Oregon border; my editor at Harvard Business School Press, Kirsten Sandberg, resides in both Boston and New York; my researchers, Thomas Bindley, Pamela Kirkbride, and Julie Kordestani work out of the McKenna Group's offices in Palo Alto; my agent, Rafe Sagalyn, attends his computer near Washington D.C.; and my advisor and friend Ann Dilworth lives in Los Angeles and Santa Fe. I work mainly from my homes in Silicon Valley and Carmel, California.

I have ISDN connections in both houses, and I can get onto the Internet quickly to track down facts, articles, home pages, and a variety of other things. Approvals for material quoted in this book have been sent via fax and e-mail, and speedily returned. The fax was necessary because permission to quote from interviews still requires a *real* signature.

All of this was not without its trials and tribulations. We worked through computer viruses; changes of Internet service providers, digital links, and routers; dysfunctional servers; AOL access problems; and lost files accounted for by this clear-as-mud message from our computers: "A Type 1 error has occurred." But we did better than just survive all that our tools inflicted on us. I don't see how, without them, we could have completed the work on this book in less than a year. My thanks go to those who made this fascinating era of communication possible and particularly to my good friends at BBN, who helped to start it all (www.bbn.com).

Like any author, I am indebted to many, many friends and associates. Cheryll Barron worked with me on the ideas and manuscript from the beginning. We have been talking to each other since her days as a journalist covering high technology and Silicon Valley for the *Economist* and *Business Week*. As her next major project after the book she wrote on the entrepreneurial Napa wine community, *Dreamers of the Valley of Plenty* (Scribners, 1995), this work received all her creative energies.

Several people reviewed early drafts and made valuable recommendations. They were Rich Melmon, one of my partners and an associate for many years; Bill Miller, former president of SRI International and a professor at the Stanford Business School—a mentor of many years' standing; Tom Kosnick, professor of technology marketing at both Stanford and Harvard—and one of the few academics I know who has dedicated his scholarly energies to the understanding and advancement of technology marketing.

Hal Feeney of Pathfinders Research (www.pathfinder-research.com), my longtime running friend and one of the first marketing managers at Intel's microprocessor operation, helped me with the topic of semiconductors and chips. Don Keithly, vice president of J. D. Power & Associates, an idea-sharing compatriot for many years, reviewed my thoughts on the auto industry. Thanks to my good friend and comrade Stepan Pachikov, founder of Paragraph International, I have been introduced to the wonderful world of virtual reality.

The people I interviewed for the book were generous with both their ideas and their time. It is unfortunate that I was unable to use all the information from these conversations, because everyone I talked to had so much experience and wisdom to offer. Bill Campbell, president and CEO of Intuit; Steve Jobs, cofounder of Apple and chairman of Pixar; Joel Birnbaum, senior vice president of R&D and head of HP Labs; Dennis Jones, the much acclaimed chief information officer of FedEx; and Dave Power, founder of J. D. Power & Associates, are all friends who have helped me with my previous books and who lent their wisdom to this effort. Carmine Villani, Kim Polese, and Deborah McWhinney are very talented real time advocates. I am sure they will continue to be leaders in their industries who will change the rules of business to accommodate both new technology and the customer well into the twenty-first century.

I had the pleasure and privilege of interviewing three other remarkable people, Edward (Ted) Shortliffe, professor of medicine and computer science at Stanford; Bill Fields, former CEO and inventive business leader of one of the most successful real time organizations, Blockbuster Entertainment; Mike Homer, vice president of marketing, Netscape; and Zvi Alon, president of NetManage (www.netmanage.com), which was the fastest-growing company in Silicon Valley in 1996.

I am indebted to my partners at the McKenna Group (www.mckenna-group.com) and the Market Relations Group (www.marketrelations.com) for their many ideas and stories and for letting me take the time to pound the computer keyboard. Finally, I must thank my wife, Dianne, who sits beside me at her computer in our home office and who provided ideas and clippings (she reads incessantly), reviewed chapters, and has helped me infuse the "wisdom of the real world" into all my projects throughout our thirty-seven years together. (Being not nearly as patient with technology or service as I am, she gives me a real time view of consumer behavior.)

I would like to have interviewed many more people, and used much more from the voluminous files and information I have collected over the past five years on the subject of this book, but I didn't have the time.

REAL TIME

INTRODUCTION

A man or a woman suddenly thrust into this world would have to dodge houses and buildings. For all is in motion. Houses and apartments, mounted on wheels, go careening through Bahnhofplatz and race through the narrows of Marktgasse, their occupants shouting from second-floor windows. The Post Bureau doesn't remain on Postgasse, but flies through the city

The Collapse of Time and Space

on rails, like a train....When a person comes out of his front door at sunrise, he hits the ground running, catches up with his office building, hurries up and down flights of stairs, works at a desk propelled in circles, gallops home at the end of the day....Why such a fixation on speed? Because in this world time passes more slowly for people in motion. Thus everyone travels at high velocity, to gain time.

—ALAN LIGHTMAN, *Einstein's Dreams*, 1993

TIME ONCE SEEMED the most reliable dimension guiding life on earth. Time was a matter of the sun passing over the meridian to mark yet another day, and life in relation to greater and smaller fragments of time had a similar evenness, a reassuring predictability. Things took just so long. Everyone counted on it. The notion of what you could accomplish in an hour or an afternoon was roughly as fixed and immutable as the nine-odd months between the conception and birth of a human being.

No more. A sense of time speeded up has become pervasive as we close out the century. Our appetite for speed is insatiable. Our preoccupation with time so relentless that it is playfully explored not just in science fiction but in novels in the literary mainstream. Faster is no longer enough. The search for the instantaneous and simultaneous has become the 1990s equivalent of the quest for the Holy Grail.

My personal index of the change in our perception of time takes me back to childhood family vacations in the early 1950s. We traveled from Pittsburgh to Lake Erie, little more than a hundred miles away, yet the trip required such enormous planning and preparation that it might have been a military exercise. My father spent at least one day making sure that our car, a 1937 Buick, was in the best possible working condition. That was because we usually left on weekends, when, thanks to the blue laws of the era, garages as well as grocery stores and all other business enterprises were closed. For days my mother shopped for and arranged all the clothes a family of seven boys would need. In the hours before we left, she packed bags and made lunches and brewed coffee for our meal en route.

These yearly journeys were pleasant, and I have many fond memories of them. But it often took longer to prepare for the vacation than to actually take it. The trip to Lake Erie was not just a journey of physical distance; it was also a journey of perception.

Today, often at a moment's notice and with no preparation, I drive a hundred miles to have lunch or breakfast with a client in San Francisco. Frequently I travel to Dallas, New York, or Tokyo, thousands of miles away, for a two-hour meeting and return within forty-eight hours. Like most everyone else, when on a trip I expect to do a lot more than just get from one place to another. I no longer experience a journey's duration as mere travel time but time to read or write, work on my portable computer, watch a movie, eat a three-course microwave dinner, make telephone calls, send a fax, or perhaps listen to music. Everything is designed to make travel not feel like travel. The complexity and effort of travel are made transparent as time and space are transformed. Having technology at our fingertips makes us more productive. But it also presents us with the challenge of cramming in yet more, of accounting for every second. Whether in our offices, our cars, or our kitchens, we are aware that time is money. Time is precious. Time waits for no one. Even today's teenagers, carrying beepers and cellular phones, reflect these proliferating, potent truths. Using the alphanumeric capability of their pagers, teens commonly answer demands on their time with 24*7, meaning: I am booked twenty-four hours a day, seven days a week.

In the world at large, in the space of a mere decade, we have witnessed many unexpected turns of events: the collapse of the

Berlin Wall and the Soviet Union, the rise of China as a world trading power, the exploding bubble of the Japanese economic miracle, the demise of the Democratic Party's forty-year dominance of the U.S. Congress, the transformation of Vietnam from adversary to U.S. trading partner, the embrace of peace by Yasser Arafat and Yitzhak Rabin, the assassination of Rabin, the displacement of uplifting images of Olympic winter sports in Sarajevo with a savage ethnic war, and the Separatist revolt in Quebec. During this same brief time span, the term *Internet* became a household word.

Racing past us like simulations of warp-speed travel, these events filled the media and our lives, conditioning our view of the world around us. Those of us in business must keep reminding ourselves that this supercharged world is the marketplace, a marketplace in which the ticking of "real time" technologies is teaching the consumer to expect and demand immediate satisfaction.

We Are Resetting Our Clocks to Real Time

Imagine a world in which time seems to vanish and space seems completely malleable. Where the gap between need or desire and fulfillment collapses to zero. Where distance equals a microsecond in lapsed connection time. A virtual world created at your command. Imagine a world in which everything you do, from work to education, is clothed as an entertainment-like experience, veiled by technology so subtle and transparent that you have no idea it is there at all. Habits, attitudes, opinions, preferences, expectations, demands, perceptions, and needs all adapt unwittingly to an environment in which immediacy rules.

All of this may sound like material for a science fiction thriller. But it is very nearly the world we are living in today.

Technology is transforming our existence in profound ways, and the pace of change is speeding up, not slowing down. Almost all technology today is focused on compressing to zero the amount of time it takes to acquire and use information, to learn, to make decisions, to initiate action, to deploy resources, to innovate. When action and response are simultaneous, we are in *real time*.

For managers all over the world, the buzz is about time to market, just-in-time manufacturing, quick time, Internet time, time-based management. In companies as in life, we seem to be feeling the strain of an evolutionary resetting of some internal, organic clock.

In 1995, scientists discovered the existence of "clock" genes in a group of worms known as nematodes. A research team at McGill University (www.mcgill.ca) in Montreal found that artificially induced mutations in these genes altered the frequency with which the nematodes ate and digested food and the rate at which they swam. The scientists tentatively concluded that the worms' clock genes work together as a kind of master timepiece, synchronizing all their life functions and their interaction with their surroundings. Today, with our own persistent and universal sense of warped time, the reorchestrative possibilities for nematode life seem closely analogous to those for human beings.

Our Changing Frame of Reference

Real time is what I am calling our sense of ultracompressed time and foreshortened horizons in these years of the millennial countdown. The change in our consciousness of time is the creation of ubiquitous programmable technology producing results at the click of a mouse or the touch of a button or key. Real time occurs when time and distance vanish, when action and response are simultaneous.

Many real time processes and activities are obvious. Most are not. We experience real time while watching live TV coverage of an event on the other side of the globe or while withdrawing money at an ATM. We experience real time when our credit card is verified in seconds, when we check our blood pressure at home. These instances of instant satisfaction change our frame of reference. They provide different patterns and signals for setting expectations and for judging what is reality, what is truth or fiction, what is good or bad service, what is satisfaction. The cultural and value-laden patterns of our society change as we are taught by our environment to adapt to new ways of doing things.

We all now expect to be able to dial directly to establish a telephone connection with almost any place in the world in seconds; to scan galaxies of information on the Internet in minutes; to establish our creditworthiness in the seconds it takes to slide a plastic card through a slot; to test on our own the level of glucose or cholesterol in our blood; to administer pregnancy tests with home diagnostic kits; to send and receive overnight packages from London or Tokyo; to fax letters to friends in Reykjavik and Manila; commission customized shirts and suits to be delivered in a week; to bank twenty-four hours a day; to turn board meetings into teleconferences of directors scattered over three continents; to follow O. J. Simpson as he flees in his white Bronco; to watch a war in progress in the Middle East.

> "Any technology gradually creates a totally new human environment."
>
> —MARSHALL MCLUHAN, *The Medium Is the Message,* 1967

You might reasonably object that the phenomenon I'm calling real time is actually more like unreal time. Its reframing of the familiar has much in common with the radical conceptual shift in twentieth-century physics toward the realm of quantum mechanics, in which subatomic matter is seen to act like both waves and particles and to be in more than one place at a time. In any case, real time is a phrase I have borrowed from computer culture, in which the usual meanings of words are almost routinely altered if not reversed—where "default" is taken to mean standard; "dedicated" means restricted; and "icon," reduced to one of its many meanings, means symbol. (See *Free On-line Dictionary of Computing* at www.instantweb.com/foldoc).

Originally, real time meant enormous computer power capable of instantaneous input and output response. The computer executed instructions as they were generated. The original impetus for this rapid program execution came from military applications such as fighter aircraft, where human reflexes were simply too slow to direct them.

In my use of the term, *real time* applies not to any device but to the technologically transformed context of everything we do. Real time is characterized by the shortest possible lapse between idea and action; between initiation and result. In the context of business, a real time experience is created from self-service and self-satisfaction by customers. It is instant response.

On the cusp of the age of real time, technological progress looks as if it is accomplished by hidden catalytic agents. The world as we know it is being changed subtly beneath familiar surfaces. Cellular phones are taking the wild out of wilderness: climbers phone home from the slopes of Mt. Everest; hikers, hunters, and Boy Scouts dial out for directions rather than navigate for themselves. The catalytic agents behind these modifications of our experience are all born of information technology. They all love speed. They all seek real time.

This is an experience of time shaped by the proliferation of a variety of communications technologies and a myriad of chip-size computers embedded in devices that are everywhere around us, from the moment we open our eyes in the morning. The average American home today has hundreds of intelligent microchips executing computing, controlling, and programming tasks, not just in personal computers but in VCRs, television sets, microwave ovens, power tools, thermostats, security systems, telephones, answering machines, calculators, fax machines, pocket calculators, wristwatches, alarm clocks, portable and stationary tape and disc players, baby monitors and stereo systems, as well as in dozens of other gadgets and countless toys.

The Future Is Out, Now Is In

Close to three decades ago, in *Future Shock*, Alvin Toffler anticipated the waves of trauma, anxiety, and panic that the riptide of the technological revolution, with its accelerated pace of change, would set off. Toffler clearly communicated how difficult it would be to live in a real time world, one in which surprises lurk around every corner. To the extent that we cannot see up ahead, he warned, our ability to cope with the future diminishes. As he put it,

> *Whether the problem is that of driving a car down a crowded street, piloting a plane...or dealing with interpersonal difficulties, performance improves when an individual knows what to expect next.*[1]

As much as I admire Toffler and his rationale, I believe that a quarter-century after his prescient work, we owe ourselves a constructive consideration of the possibilities of life lived on fast-forward. We will increasingly find that the technologies of speed will not give us the time to see or plan beyond the horizon. We will have to think and act in real time. We cannot choose to do otherwise. We can and must get better at what we do best. Adaptability and a love of speed are quintessentially American qualities and must be reckoned among our finest comparative advantages. It is no accident that the land of the ninety-second McDonald's hamburger, instant tanning lotion, and self-service hotel checkout is also home to more personal computers, more networked computers, and more wireless communications devices than any other nation.

The Benefit of Short-Term Thinking

Companies large and small are playing to classic American strengths when they do not embrace the technologies of speed as ends in themselves but work to comprehend the widest and most subtle consequences of their adoption. One of these consequences, I believe, is an even greater orientation toward the short term. Never mind if it has become a cliché to accuse American business and Wall Street of too much short-term thinking. The positive side of this trait is a hair-trigger responsiveness as measured against the standards of European or Japanese companies.

For sure, there are times when a focus on more distant horizons richly benefits other business cultures at our expense. For instance, in some boom cycles, American semiconductor companies have lost market share to Japanese competitors that, with an eye to future demand, invested more heavily in production capacity. At these times, CEOs of American chip makers have cursed the financial markets for making it impossible (given the certainty with which plummeting stock ratings follow diminished short-term profitability) to lay on all the extra capacity their companies are capable of. Yet the relentless application of Wall Street's quarter-by-quarter yardstick for success and competitiveness also accounts for the unmatched pace of innovation among American chip makers. For all businesses, the speed of change, competitive response, and adaptation is interpreted by Wall Street as evidence of savvy management.

Admittedly, companies in Japan, Europe, and other parts of the world are also speeding up their operations and developing innovative ways to address the real time marketplace. But my focus in this book is the American marketplace. This is because America presents a real time microcosm in which we might first expect to see adopted— technologically as well as socially—the concepts and practices that will soon be diffused throughout the world.

America is a microcosm of the real time concepts and practices that will soon be diffused throughout the world.

American companies are actually evidence that an emphasis on short-term considerations is the best guarantor of long-term strength and competitiveness. For this seeming paradox there is a parallel in long-distance running. You do not train for marathons by running marathons every day but by running shorter distances and sprints. Sprinting improves control of breathing as well as muscle tone and endurance. This training prepares the runner for the long haul. The pressure for short-term results also goes hand in hand with an attitude prized in American industry. This is pragmatism, or the attitude encapsulated in the saying, "The best is the enemy of the good."

In analyzing the reasons for the huge lead American companies have over the Japanese in software, for example, Stanford University researchers mentioned this cultural bias, among other factors. "Good enough" quality, they said, is acceptable in the United States. In an industry in which time to market is critical, Japanese companies are handicapped by a culture that exalts perfectionism. American companies believe in getting that new product out the door as fast and as cheap and possible, opting to back it up with a variety of technical and support services. Japanese companies delay product introductions for the sake of extensive quality assurance and testing procedures. And the Stanford team's overall conclusion? "The U.S. economic, organizational and cultural context fosters adaptation during periods of extremely rapid change in technology."[2] (See the Stanford Computer Industry Project, or SCIP, at www-scip.stanford.edu/scip.)

In real time, the best is the enemy of the good.

Instant Success Takes Time

While many companies are speeding up their various internal processes, minimizing procedures, and eliminating costly delays, application of the most powerful real time concept—using an information feedback loop from customers and market infrastructure to design and service, and back out again—has barely begun. Most approaches today are fragmented, not part of a unified business strategy. Real time is emphatically not about simple acceleration or merely doing faster what organizations have done before. Nor is it specifically about the Internet, although the World Wide Web is unquestionably a real time technology.

Companies best equipped for the twenty-first century will consider investment in real time systems as essential to maintaining their competitive edge and keeping their customers. By this I mean that they will use information and telecommunications technology to respond to changing circumstances and, even more important, customer expectations within the smallest possible lapse of time. They will understand that real time is about exceptional responsiveness. They will understand that customers' expectations are being reset for hyperaccelerated, if not immediate, company response, no matter what they happen to be buying. The competitive environment will no longer tolerate slow response or delayed decision making.

Creating a real time organization will be similar to the exercise of implementing total quality management (TQM). In the 1980s, many companies striving to improve the quality of their products and services discovered that attention to quality was not just a discrete step in the management process. The importance of quality had to be embedded in the thinking of every person in the organization. Implementing TQM was and still is a difficult and challenging process. So is deploying real time processes and systems.

Managing the information technology behind the ultra-responsiveness of real time is not a job that can be delegated to a chief information officer or any other kind of specialist. It requires total management engagement. This is not to say that leaders of successful real time organizations will have to turn themselves into computer programmers but that they will have to grasp and act on the ramifications of real time.

How can organizations be prepared to reconceptualize what they do in this way? First, by exposing people at all levels of the company to examples of successful adaptations to real time thinking and operation: ways of developing channels for interactive relationships with customers and building customer communities; using information technology networks to generate and test new ideas and innovate faster; educating and training customers in new and labor-saving ways of accomplishing their ends by building instructions into technologies located in or accessible from their houses or offices or even cars.

I recently gave a talk to a group of visiting Japanese businessmen and was asked this question: "In the year 2010, will the computer or the TV set be *the* information appliance in the home?" This is a matter hotly debated in the communications field, the assumption being that anyone who knows the answer to the question will simply build the right product before anyone else does. "The device will be the microwave oven," I said. My audience smiled. Some even chuckled aloud. I assured them that I was not joking. If information is piped into the home and distributed like electricity, I explained, then any device can become a smart information appliance. Julia Child could pop up on the microwave flat panel screen to advise on the latest recipe for pasta just downloaded from a database in Italy.

Real time wrecks hierarchical organizations by making possible instant access to activities of all stripes—anywhere, anytime, all the time. Instead of fruitlessly trying to predict the future course of a competitive or market trend, customer behavior or demand, managers should be trying to find and deploy all the tools that will enable them, in some sense, to be ever-present, ever-vigilant, and ever-ready in the brave new marketplace in gestation, where information and knowledge are ceaselessly exchanged. Managers dedicated to making the future happen will, in some ways, be preparing for the eventuality of anything.

For the printed page, time stops. For the real time world we live in, knowledge is dynamic. My purpose in writing this book is to raise questions, create discussion, and think in new terms. To keep the information in this book fresh and current, you can

Keeping *Real Time*, real time

tune into the McKenna Group Web site for new case studies, points of view, discussions, and comments about *Real Time* applications and businesses.

WWW.MCKENNA-GROUP.COM

As miniaturization advanced with lightning rapidity, as computer capacity soared and prices per function plunged, small cheap powerful microcomputers began to sprout everywhere. Every branch factory, laboratory, sales office or engineering department claimed its own.

—ALVIN TOFFLER, *The Third Wave*, 1980

Bits and Bytes in Perpetual Motion

Digital information is forever. It doesn't deteriorate and requires little in the way of material media.

—ANDREW GROVE, chairman, Intel Corporation, 1996

TECHNOLOGY AND SOCIETY shape and reshape
each other ceaselessly, like tireless meshing
gears in a perpetual motion machine. This
is nothing new. Yet in the twentieth century the
scale of the interchange and its consequences
for people and social institutions have far
exceeded anything seen in previous eras.

The New Technology: Shaping the Social Fabric

Over the last hundred years, the idea of
fomenting common aspirations within
a mass culture or "consumer society"
was inspired by the technologies of
production and communication. As
early as 1903, the metaphor of mass
production had insinuated itself into
social thinking. "The public school
system of this country," wrote one cor-
respondent of the *New York Times* that
year, "is a great factory, where the raw
material from foreign lands is manufactured into patriotic American citizens,
with the language, the sentiments, the
patriotism, the manners, the customs, and
the National aspirations of Americans."[1]

Technology's effects on us today are different from those of the industrial revolution.
They are more democratic, more personal,
more subtle and profound. They are changing
our very perceptions and judgments of value, our
loyalties and relationships. They are changing *who we*

are, even as we casually press each new technological marvel into service, taking it for granted.

The signs are all around us. They are reflected in two stories on a single page of a recent issue of the *New York Times* (www.nytimes.com). One reported on the results of an opinion poll by the advertising agency Saatchi & Saatchi, in which women were asked for their views on the depiction of their sex in TV commercials. Participants in the survey particularly admired an Apple Computer ad in which a woman shown working at home on a PC, juggling the demands of children and a ringing telephone, puts together a report that later wins praise from her boss. The survey's supervisor at Saatchi said that the participating women liked the depiction of "the improvisational woman, who makes it up as she goes along and has got it together." They saw the commercial as needed encouragement during a period of turmoil, inordinate time pressure, and insecurity caused by women's changing roles.

But it was technology—from modern appliances to the birth control pill—that gave women the option to alter their roles and stretch their definitions of themselves. In the age of real time, given the opportunity to pack even more into a day and live out still other identities, most women will take it. They will want devices like the one that was the subject of the other story in the *Times* that day: a new AT&T cellular telephone with a tiny three-line display screen, integrating voice and Internet services, capable of browsing the World Wide Web, and permitting absolutely no excuse for not answering e-mail from anywhere. They will want the rival technologies and products that AT&T's competition will offer, catering to their desire to stretch even farther (www.attws.com).[2]

Technology alters semiconscious and subconscious notions of community and heritage. In his 1990 book *Time Passages*, George Lipsitz observes:

Time, history and memory become qualitatively different concepts in a world where electronic mass communication is possible. Instead of relating to the past through a shared sense of place or ancestry, consumers of electronic mass media can experience a common heritage with people they have never seen; they can acquire memories of a past to which they have no geographical or biological connection. This capacity of electronic mass communication to transcend time and space creates instability by disconnecting people from past traditions, but it also liberates people by making the past less determinate of experiences in the present.[3]

A Shift to People Power

Most uncanny, perhaps, is the link between the evolution of computers and the shift in the self-image of two successive generations of Americans. In the era of big, impersonal corporations and big, remote, mainframe computers housed in sterile rooms—a time in which the managerial ideal was the trusty, robot-like Organization Man—alienated workers felt they were treated like numbers on computer cards. The next generation, benefiting from educational opportunities unknown to its parents, refused to accept these metaphors as models for their own lives. Explaining the underlying cause of the rebellion in a speech on the Berkeley campus in 1964, the student leader Mario Savio said, "[It is] the alienation that students feel from what is a knowledge factory....You're processed. You become a number on a set of file cards that go through an IBM machine." Student protest placards of that year read, "I am a student. Do not fold, bend, or mutilate."

The personal computer, a symbol of egalitarianism and individualism, was the brainchild of that same counterculture revolution, whose rallying cry was, "Power to the people!" Here was an example of society reforming technology. Apple Computer cofounder Steve Jobs famously warned, "Never trust a computer you can't lift," precisely echoing the cultural revolutionaries' motto: "Never trust anyone over thirty."

Yet technology does not always suit society's wants and expectations so neatly. It has brought distressing social fragmentation. More and more, an expanding range of real time communications capabilities puts people from all walks of life on call twenty-four hours a day, like emergency room doctors. Advanced communications are breaching sovereign borders and putting unprecedented powers into the hands of individuals capable of executing transactions and moving various forms of information and capital in and out of markets on a global scale. The gap widens between the world's information elite and information have-nots, who have only limited contact with computers and networks, or none. Half of the world's population has yet to make a telephone call. There are serious and fully warranted concerns about the future effects of information and communications technologies on society.

The PC is a symbol of egalitarianism and individualism.

A License to Speed

Unlike the inventions of the industrial revolution or the many technological innovations that followed it, real time technologies have permeated society like clandestine catalytic agents, their speed and media of transmission freeing them from past constraints. Until the mid- to late 1970s, large companies, big government, and a handful of powerful educational institutions largely controlled the distribution of technological innovation.

Government had a hand in establishing and running the railroads, telegraph service, radio and television broadcasting, and the pharmaceutical and mainframe computer industries. Most significant technologies of the twentieth century have been regulated in some form or other. Indeed, government permission is required to operate most of these technologies. For instance, I need a license to drive a car or to run a radio or TV station. As a result, innovation seeped out slowly and deliberately.

In contrast, the makers and users of personal computers today do not need a license to operate; nor do the millions of Internet surfers and users of fax machines. Indeed, types and forms of computing and communication are changing so rapidly that the regulators at the Federal Communications Commission, as well as most other large established institutions, are hard pressed to keep up with them. Modems, satellite dishes, and fax machines proliferate, and information moves back and forth seamlessly across the borders of even the most closed societies. As a result, the rapid changes and effects of real time technologies are rapidly absorbed and adapted by those who use them.

No agent of the industrial revolution could have insinuated itself into the culture as stealthily as the PC.

No agent of the industrial revolution could have insinuated itself into the culture so stealthily. I can still vividly recall driving along the Boulevard of the Allies by the Monongahela River in Pittsburgh in the 1940s and 1950s. The steel mills and their blast furnaces lined the waterfront like visions from Dante's *Inferno*, molten metal poured from ladles reflected against the evening sky in explosions of crimson light. There was no escaping the physical evidence of the mass production process—railcars and trucks loaded with steel, polluted rivers, and murky skies.

Technology Diffusion and the Pace of Change

| Technology Innovation | Institutional Control | Slow, Controlled Diffusion | Social Acceptance and Change |

1875–1975

| Technology Innovation | Rapid Market Diffusion | Social Acceptance and Change | Institutional Acceptance |

1975–Present

Once technology was under the control of established institutions. Big government, business, and education played a major role in both its creation and diffusion. No more. The speed and the ubiquity of communication move ideas, services, opinions, and money faster than institutions are capable of responding. We people are able to absorb and adapt to these changes as they occur, while institutions struggle to keep up.

The Silent Power of Silicon

While the steam engines and colossal mills that moved people off farms and into factories announced their presence with grinding and hissing, the silicon chips responsible for the information revolution express their intelligence through the silent and imperceptible movements of electrons. It is as if a new dimension has been given to Adam Smith's idea of the "invisible hand" of capitalism, working toward universal economic well-being.

In the pathways of the microchip, also known as a silicon chip or semiconductor, embedded elements hustle electrons through decision-making "gates"—which work in Boolean logic, at the level of 1s and 0s, to say "and," "or," or "not"—and on to other chips, where they will be stored or used to trigger or amplify action. There are chips that produce sound, video images, and laser light; chips that calculate, remember, regulate, amplify, control, and communicate. Though their variety is endless, they have in common ease of integration and their consequent capacity to speed up what were once discrete tasks.

For me, there is an abiding sense of the miraculous about the embedded channels in the microchips through which electrons move at speeds of millionths of a second. The state of the art in the so-called line widths of these channels is *submicron* technology. A micron is one-millionth of a meter, or the width of a human hair. Chips can contain up to several million submicron pathways moving information in the form of electrons from input to output. In between, more than a million logic gates, or decision points, are jammed onto a piece of silicon little bigger than a contact lens. Semiconductors are manufactured in batches on silicon wafers containing hundreds of discrete chips, resulting in a clockwork decline in production costs at the rate of 30 percent a year, for one year after another. For more than three decades, the cost/performance ratio of chips has adhered to Moore's Law, which refers to the staggering, steadily exponential advance in the logic density of microchips: their raw processing power doubles every eighteen months.

The physical and psychological distance between this technology's forges and the rest of society—quite unlike Pittsburgh steel making—can be illustrated in the very pronunciation of the word *silicon*. A number of people—news commentators, politicians, actors—mispronounce the name of this basic raw material of the information revolution. Silicon is a derivative of silica, the most abundant element in nature next to oxygen. People in the semiconductor industry—the industry that gave Silicon Valley its name—have long pronounced the word as *silikin*; *Webster's*, on the other hand, rules that the *con* in *silicon* should rhyme with the *bon* in *carbon*. Neither source supplies any ground for the popular confusion in which *silicon* is pronounced as a homonym for *silicone*, a synthetic petrochemical and the stuff of controversial breast implants. Yet whether one hears *silicone, silicon,* or *silikin* in reference to computers or communications technology, the concept itself is proliferating and its meaning is clear: advanced technology inside.

But then part of the entertainment of my thirty-plus years in Silicon Valley has come from observing both the development of information technologies and their rapid sifting into every crevice of a society largely oblivious to them. I cannot say whether I am more astonished by the dimensions of that obliviousness or by the phenomenal computational power and speed that silicon chips have made possible.

Today's laptop computers deliver more than a hundred times the performance of the typical engineering workstations of 1985. In a mere greeting card, a singing or talking microchip carries more computing moxie than those first computers of the 1950s, even though their difference in size is proportionately greater than that between a hot dog stand and a skyscraper. Microchips are the hardware undergirding the rising fuel efficiency of cars, the instantaneous transfer of funds between continents, the digital music so uncannily true to the auditory nuances of live concerts, the criminal fingerprint and photographic records relayed to police officers in their cars, and a grocery store's ability to manage 30,000 or more items on its shelves.

But the products with the capacity most radically enlarged by microchips—those of the communications industry—have been spawning yet another societal sea change. This one is already dwarfing the information revolution in the scope of its ramifications and reverberations.

From Computing to Communicating

Communications systems are most prone to being transformed by progress in computers because of the huge overlap between their respective means and ends. Computers work by manipulating and communicating digital data composed of bits that can represent almost any form of information—voice, data, text, sound, graphics, video, touch, pressure, heat, and light. Until recently, computers were principally used as machines working with other machines, while communications technologies directly served people as channels uniting them. With the advent of distributed computing, digital data can now move over networks, including networks stretching from continent to continent, exactly like data inside a single computer. By the same token, the critical components of modern communications systems are now computers: for instance, the modern switch managing the millions of phone call connections at your local telephone company is a digital computer.

Software and silicon might be seen as the yin and yang of real time. Software plays a vital role in digital technology by providing rapid adaptability, or programmability, for almost any application, including many in communications. It can even extend the life of older technologies or rapidly upgrade them. For the past hundred years, copper wire has been installed on telephone poles and in the ground. Today, software artifacts such as data packets and software techniques such as data compression make it possible for bits to move at lightning speed over those wires, which are now positively geriatric.

A Global Nervous System

Within the next decade or so, satellite systems will house chip-sized digital computers capable of moving voice, data, and video bits to the remotest regions of China, Africa, and Borneo. The result will be explosive growth in demand for digital technology. Competition and technology will drive costs down as a global "communications highway" emerges. Communication content as varied as the people who have access to this infrastructure—and residing in millions of computers on every continent—will move around as if in a single giant information processor. As Scott McNealy, president of Sun Microsystems (www.sun.com), correctly prophesied more than a decade ago, "The network *is* the computer."[4] This vision is now taking shape around the planet.

Soon, global inter-networking—networks linked to other networks, like the Internet—with hybrid fiber, coaxial cable, cellular, and satellite transmissions will be responsible for unimaginable leaps in "bandwidth," which is to say, communications capacity. Computer networks that today transmit data at megabits (millions) a second will soon be graduating to a rate of gigabits (billions) a second, creating a universe of "broad band" communications. Consider, for scale, that the human voice communicates at a snail's pace of about 55 bits a second.

"The network *is* the computer."

—Scott McNealy

Businesses, organizations, governments, and individuals are finding the quickly growing World Wide Web to be a rapid and economical way of communicating to their employees, partners, and customers. Databases that once were accessible to only a few are now on-line, bringing untold volumes of information—ranging from sports statistics, news articles, government demographic data, library holdings, and tourist information to newspaper and magazine subscriptions, astronomy pictures, rock concerts, and Shakespeare's complete works—to broad communities of interest. As more and more computers are added to the network, they create increased demand by adding a new community of people interested in accessing the particular information provided. The "pipeline," or network, does not have the capacity, or bandwidth, to handle the millions of simultaneous transactions that may occur. As a result, computer and telecommunications companies are feverishly working to develop new software for compressing data and higher-speed chips and computers to move bits faster. The entire "Internet industry" is running on real time in an effort to put into place an efficient infrastructure with the hope that the "content" made available will have value.

What does all this gee-whizzery amount to? Once, computers chiefly ground away at numbers that they then organized, stored, and printed out in reams of categorized data: lists, payroll records, accounting data, and inventory reports for a few

Internet Hosts, 1989–1997

Hosts are the computer server, filled with various types of information and linked together creating the World Wide Web (www). Most are freely accessible. Surfing this information highway, one can access millions of documents, photos, books, and movies as well as e-mail friends and associates anywhere, anytime.

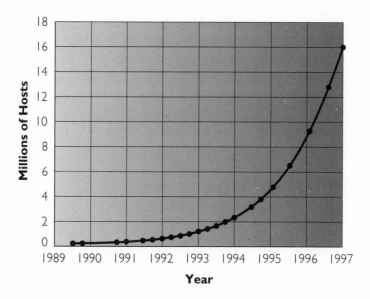

Source: A. M. Rutkowski, General Magic, Inc., Network Wizards, January 1997.
(www.genmagic.com and www.nw.com)

managers to peruse. As bandwidth expands, images of extraordinary complexity will be transmittable: you could say that a picture or graph will in the future be worth not one hundred words but one hundred *million* words. Now, computer power at the service of communications delivers information where and when it is needed and in a form chosen by the user. Soon managers interacting with each other with unprecedented intellectual and emotional intimacy will turn bits into ideas, action, and response.

For the consumer, this phase of technological progress will serve interests and desires closer to the human heart—like the real time news coverage that satellites have made possible. People all around the globe were able to share the excitement of the crowds tearing down the Berlin Wall and the passion of the students striking blows for freedom in Tiananmen Square. Thanks to satellites, Himalayan tribes in the almost inaccessible area of Arunachal in India now watch soap operas and other television programming from America and Bombay. In "Far Northeast India, Mountain Tribes Meet the World," an article in the *Washington Post* (www.washingtonpost.com), writer Molly Moore recounted one instance of intergenerational conflict caused by this new electronic propinquity, as told by a disgruntled Nishi tribesman: "My son insists that I wear trousers and says I should get rid of my headdress and cut my hair."[5]

Satellite television has introduced foreign programming into nearly 20 million Indian households, whose choice of TV fare only ten years ago was limited to a single, dull government-run channel called Doordarshan. There are more than forty channels on tap in India today, and more than a hundred more are expected to be launched by the year 2000 by international communications leaders such as Sony, Columbia, Sky, Star, Time-Warner, HBO, and Disney, either in partnership with Indian companies or independently.

Indian TV personality Vibha Chhabra notes one of the remarkable effects of this evolution: the liberalization of sexuality—or at least of the willingness to talk about it. India, the country that gave the world the Kama Sutra, the fourth-century guide to love making, in subsequent centuries experienced something like an eclipse of eroticism. For most of this century, even kissing has been prohibited in Indian movies by government order. Now, thanks to sky-based video networks, all this is changing.

On Sunday nights, viewers all across India turn on their television sets to *Purush Kshetra*, India's first sexual-advice television show.

Confessions on everything from sexual dysfunction to female orgasm are on public display. Judging from the fan mail it receives, the program has succeeded in unleashing the Indian viewer's libido. What would a visitor from a previous generation, brought up on conservative Victorian values, make of a whole population absorbed in contemplation of flickering images communicating information and advise on the passions of love and lust?[6]

Years before the collapse of the Soviet Union, former premier Mikhail Gorbachev said, "No country can today isolate its economic, political, or social environment from any other nation." Thanks to satellites, his remark has proved even more prescient than he might have imagined. Satellites have had an extraordinary influence on business and consumers over the last twenty years. And we have hardly seen anything yet. In the next decade, some 1,700 satellites will be launched in space,[7] creating the potential for more than 3 billion people to view CNN (www.cnn.com), make a phone call, tap into the information highway, or watch reruns of *Seinfeld* and *The X-Files*. Assimilation will be swift. Our modern communications system is the result of more than half a century of planting copper wires in the ground, over our heads, and in our walls. The twenty-first century's infrastructure of satellites, ground stations, and wireless networks is being put in place in a fraction of that time.

Computer nerds and neophytes alike are being united in quasi-communities founded on whizzing bits. A global nervous system is being assembled, linking ideas, information, images, and the cultural repositories of nations—the whole Pandora's box of human affairs—that can be tapped into by anyone with a telephone, a TV, a personal computer, or a device that combines all three. Technology trends of recent years and of today very clearly constitute the past that will serve as prologue to that future.

> **A global nervous system is being assembled that can tap into the whole Pandora's box of human affairs.**

Twenty-five years ago, there were fewer than 25,000 computers on the planet. More than 200 million computers are in use today. In the United States, the average metropolitan area has more than 50 cable and TV stations, and that number will double over the next five years. Around 1983, Europe had some 80 TV stations. It now has more than 800. Sitting at home, surfing the Internet, we can reach a bank in Helsinki (www.tradepoint.fi/info links/bankfin.html), take a math course at Washington State University (www.sci.wsu.edu/math/courses/on_line_courses.html), and scan weather patterns over East Africa (www.comet.net/weather/climate/owl_africa_climate.html-ssi). Comfortably ensconced in my home office, I have toured an exhibition of Civil War photographs at the Smithsonian in Washington, D.C. (http://lcweb.loc.gov/rr/print/), and traveled from Sri Lanka (www.tbc.gov.bc.ca/cwgames/country/SriLanka/srilanka.html) to Lithuania (http://neris.mii.lt), where I explored maps, photos, and other information on Lithuania's public access servers. I have watched, in real time, via streaming video, an eclipse of the moon (www.graham.com).

The communications revolution is tilting the balance of power from institutions to individuals. We once feared an Orwellian Big Brother. Instead, it is big institutions that are bridling at the uncontrolled and prolific dissemination of sensitive information. Empowered by the Freedom of Information Act, and with ready access to databases, journalists and private citizens alike have powerful tools for getting and using data once guarded closely by government agencies and private corporations. Stockholders have access to the CEO's salary and the perks that go with the job. They can monitor insider trading daily. Outsiders satisfy their curiosity about companies' compensation programs and competitive tactics and strategies. Hackers and computer pirates scale electronic walls to steal military secrets and can, if they choose, help themselves to more mundane information about people's spending habits, debts, traffic tickets, and medical records.

> **The communications revolution is tilting the balance of power from institutions to individuals.**

An Experiment in Direct Democracy

Radios, fax machines, satellites, and the World Wide Web are unhampered by any rusted Iron Curtain or barbed wire. In 1991, shortly after the attempted coup of the Gorbachev regime in the Soviet Union, my wife, Dianne, and I ran into an old friend and former presidential hopeful, Gary Hart, as he was shopping in London. He was on his way to Moscow to meet with the Soviet foreign minister, Eduard Shevardnadze, and asked us if we knew where he could buy a fax machine nearby. Apparently that was the one thing Shevardnadze had asked him to bring with him. Faxes and computer communications were the safest and most confidential way to maintain the links established between the many prodemocracy groups during the crisis. The only way to stay one step ahead of the Communist apparatchiks was to send information in the form of "bits" rather than by voice.

The latest wave of technological progress is making representative democracy seem increasingly unsatisfactory. Certainly, the new technologies could hasten a worldwide transition to "direct" democracy, truer to its ancient Athenian origins, in which every citizen's judgment was given equal weight in matters of government. This kind of democracy is now practiced only in Switzerland (www.vote.org/v/swiss2.htm). As noted in the *Economist*:

> *In Switzerland it is possible to insist, by collecting a modest number of signatures, that any law proposed by the government must be submitted to a vote of the whole people....Australia and some parts of the Western United States also now use referendums in a fairly regular way. There have even started to be referendums in Europe outside Switzerland.... [E]lsewhere, democracy is still stuck in a halfway house, as it were, in which the final word is delegated to the chosen few.*
>
> *...It has long been pointed out that to hold an election every few years is not only a highly imprecise way of expressing the voter's wishes (because on these rare election days he has to consider a large number of issues, and his chosen "representative" will in fact not represent him on several of them), but it is also notably loose-wristed (because the voter has little control over his representatives between elections).*[8]

In a world where politicians act only on the instructions of instantaneous public polls, we are, perhaps, moving toward a form of true citizen's government. It is not difficult to imagine a future in which voters sitting at home will be able to organize referendums, educate themselves in exhaustive detail about the pros and cons of issues, and register their votes. Will this necessarily produce a political utopia? Maybe not. It is possible to envisage a society so dominated by special interest groups that the views and votes of all the people are not, in fact, readily accepted. We may not like or adapt well to fully participative democracy. We could discover unappreciated advantages in our present form of slow-moving, deliberative, insufficiently representative democracy. We might find that in its inertia, for example, there is more than a measure of stability.

The technologies of the next century will bring more individual freedom and control. An Iron Information Curtain is unlikely.

A popular theme in news media and science fiction today stems from the fear of an atomized, disconnected society: masses of isolated people broadcasting anonymous opinions from the mouths of avatars with strange pseudonyms. I am not surprised that real time technologies are fomenting anxiety of this sort. However, I see them doing far more good for society than did the quintessential twentieth-century technologies, which were, in retrospect, highly dehumanizing. From sweatshops to HAL-like mainframe computers and atomic weapons, the technologies of the twentieth century brought in their wake the fear—and reality—of suppression, repression, and annihilation. The technologies of the next century, as far as we can tell, present the opportunity for more individual freedom and control. Although the information revolution will present its own problems, the construction of an Iron Information Curtain is unlikely.

Who Needs Vision?

Some businesspeople have no patience for this sort of wide-angled gazing at the big picture. What, they want to know, has any of it got to do with the price of eggs?

The proximate effects on business of merging computers and communications are no less remarkable for being familiar. Yet they are its least significant consequence for organizations striving to incorporate the perspectives of real time thinking into management. To be sure, linked computers control and automate manufacturing, speed the design of packaging, minimize inventories, assist automatic scheduling and distribution, and track bar codes on products at every stage in the pipeline. But the clue to computerization's most profound consequence for the business environment lies in the estimated 50,000 new products—designed, simulated, and tested with the aid of computers—that are announced every year in America, up from only a few thousand annually in 1970. These new products have sprung from a meshing of technological and social vectors that is profoundly altering the psychology of markets.

In the new reforming marketplace—just as in those countries and regions that now hold regular political referendums—choice has itself become a paramount value. Business has come a long way from Henry Ford's assembly line stamping out a one-size-fits-all Model T.

Consider a common domestic chore: buying food. As the product count in the average supermarket has risen from a few thousand in 1950 to 10,000 in 1980 to more than 30,000 today, the number of cereal brands that see at least $1 million in annual revenues has grown from 84 in 1979 to more than

150 today. There are a thousand brands of mustard, hundreds of different shapes and kinds of cookies, entire walls lined with cosmetics and dairy products, and more than a hundred brands of lipstick. The grocery store near my home recently added to its beverage aisle a section for beers from microbreweries. I counted thirty-three different labels, most of which I didn't recognize.

The computers, scanners, databases, and networks of information technology have turned the grocery store into an international food bazaar. Twenty years ago, a mainstream grocery store could not have accommodated the handful of customers who preferred pita bread to Ritz crackers. On grocery shelves today are such exotica (or what used to be exotica) as sake, lemon grass, coconut milk, several brands of black bean and soy sauce, Basmati rice, tamarind pods, bok choy, French sea salt, morels, polenta, mangoes, lavosh, and challah bread.

Managing 30,000 or more items in a grocery store has required sophisticated information and telecommunications systems. With these systems in place, a retail store can stock shelves just-in-time, quickly replacing slow-moving items and tailoring stock to local demand. But the effects of these technologies go further. Joining the dots, one can attribute the growth of megastores, even the decline of brand loyalty, to the proliferation of retail information systems.

In a curious reminder of the parallel between the counterculture and personal computer revolutions, society is changing in the same direction that technology is pushing business. The media, just as much as grocery stores, mirror the reversal of the melting pot syndrome in American culture. People of Chinese or Mexican descent tune in to radio and TV stations in their native languages, in which newspapers are published and government documents and ballots are prepared. There are more than sixty newspapers nationwide for readers of Vietnamese origin. One of the largest distributors of ethnic newspapers, Media

Masters Distribution of Queens, New York, carries more than 200 titles and makes 8,000 stops in eight different states.

A 1993 article in *Advertising Age* (www.adage.com) dispensed go-get-'em advice to marketers about grasping the revenue opportunities that lie in pandering to the tastes of recent immigrants from Eastern Europe, the Middle East, and Asia:

> When these new American Pioneers arrive, often with only what they can carry or wear, they will need food, clothing, household furnishings. As they attain their piece of the American dream, they will require bigger ticket items....Marketers must start from scratch in the language of each target market, work within the context of the original culture and formulate copy and design rooted in the culture itself. And if you end up with 10 different campaigns, so be it.[9]

Often, there are not ten different pitches for ten different ethnic groups. Instead, marketing becomes a matter of constructing a fascinating multicultural pizza. In a Nordstorm mail order clothing catalogue, for example, a beautiful black model poses beside a yellow sports car. Beneath the size and fabric information are the words of the Chinese sage Lao Tzu: "Keeping to the main road is easy, but people love to be sidetracked." A single photograph is apparently designed to appeal to women who are or would like to be young, adventurous, and sports loving; black women; Chinese Americans; women whose worldview has been conditioned by New Age or Eastern philosophy; or some combination of these.

Nonetheless, refined and high-powered computer databases increasingly allow marketers to tailor goods, services, and promotions precisely to customers' individual preferences and requirements. The result? Customers have gone from being surprised and delighted by marketers' attempts to discover what will most please them to demanding that they do nothing less—

just as in education, minorities once thrilled to have their languages on schools' curricula at all are now insisting that their children be taught the history, literature, myths, and music of their cultures of origin. Expanding customer requirements and advancing technological means of meeting them are the driving forces of real time management.

The real time message:

Society and technology are in a continual dance, each moving and swaying in response to unanticipated moves by the other. Real time technology swiftly embeds itself in everything, everywhere, profoundly affecting the marketplace and every business participating in it. To discover how best to use the new technological tools to cross traditional market or geographic boundaries, adapt their modus operandi, and still keep their customers happy, managers must first get acquainted with the dimensions of the new technological power and its incipient social effects.

Technology has intervened in the intangible, telescoping our emotions. Those antipodean states, dread and anticipation, have been practically outdated. The ordeal of dread is banished by instant full communication from anywhere to anywhere. Anticipation becomes instant gratification.

—NADINE GORDIMER, *World Link*,
May–June 1996

2

The Never Satisfied Customer

RIGHT HERE. RIGHT NOW. Tailored for me. Served up the way I like it. If the new consumer's expectations were spelled out on a billboard, that is how they would read. Top managers monotonously repeat, as if intoning mantras, that this is the age of customer service or the age of the consumer. Yet few of these managers realize what they must do for that customer to earn his or her complete approval. Consumer criteria for absolute satisfaction from supplier organizations, whether a company or a branch of government, have become so stringent as to seem unreal by the standards of the past.

Still, some of the most unlikely institutions have gotten parts of the message ahead of the rest: they have understood the need for extraordinary flexibility and have adapted accordingly, offering consumers both choice and access. One of these is a public agency upending government's reputation for sloth and rigidity. The Department of Motor Vehicles (DMV), seeking to maximize public cooperation with the enforcement of driving laws, offers some traffic offenders—as an alternative to steep fines and a hike in their auto insurance rates—a staggering array of choices for remedial instruction, known as traffic school. These are among the options available in several states to a driver who has earned, say, one too many speeding tickets: seven hours of daytime instruction on any day of the week, including Saturday and Sunday, or three and a half hours each on two consecutive weekday evenings. In California, the reforming speeder can attend any of 3,000 classrooms scattered across the state, run by certified, independent instructors (not government employees). The class offerings include those run by comedians who sugarcoat the predictable lessons with unpredictable wit and those held in pizzerias where students also get their dinner. There are the "Escuela Latina De Trafico-Espanol," an "Armenian-Persian-Spanish Classes" outfit, variations on "Finally a Gay Traffic School," budget-conscious operations such as the "Ultimate Discount and Fun Safety Traffic School," and the catchall establishment that advertises itself as "Laffs & Comedy—Low Cost—AM/PM—7 Days."

Traffic offenders of the near future can, of course, be expected to take their punishment over the Internet, from on-line schools. But the DMV had a glimmer of consumer attitudes to come way back in 1986, when it handed over the job of remedial teaching to outside contractors who, being in competition with each other, have every incentive to be accommodating.

The Conditioning of the Consumer

Choice gives the customer power. An empowered customer becomes a loyal customer by virtue of being offered products and services finely calibrated to his or her needs. That amounts to a reversal of the pattern of the past, in which consumers or users of things had to arrange their lives according to the product or service desired. People had to shop during relatively limited store hours, to buy an automobile from one of the Big Three, to make phone calls from fixed locations, to treat the office computer room like a temple, approaching it only through intermediary MIS priests.

The personal computer remains the most stunning marker for the transition, putting personal information and network access into the hands of consumers and reinforcing consumers' growing sense of autonomy by giving them access to ever more finely tuned information on which to base buying decisions. Personal computers surpassed television set sales in revenues in 1994, outpaced VCR unit sales in 1996, and are expected to outpace TV unit sales in 1997. At the time of the PC's invention in the 1970s, the idea of buying a low-cost computer for use by one person from a specialty retail store like Circuit City (www.circuitcity.com) seemed about as plausible as purchasing a personal aircraft or personal train from Sears Roebuck (www.sears.com) or JCPenney (www.jcpenney.com).

Yet the conditioning of the new, empowered consumer, expecting more or less instant gratification, took place at a steady pace over many decades. Most middle-aged adults probably have some equivalent of my first glimpse of the possibilities of real time. One summer in the early 1950s, I remember racing with my friends down to the new dry cleaner in town, in whose window flashed a big red neon sign announcing, "One Hour Shirt Cleaning." Amazed at the efficiency, we stuck our noses against the glass to watch the astonishing maneuvers of the automatic shirt-pressing machine.

Like every other technology-toned consumer, I have in the intervening years come to take for granted other marvels of compressed time: direct-dial telephone and fax services for communicating almost anywhere in the world; packages delivered overnight, with the bonus of being able to discover, at almost any time of day, the whereabouts of a parcel in transition with an 800 call to a customer service representative or with track-it-yourself software. Other time-compressed, mind-altering technologies include instantaneous, worldwide news from CNN, pagers, cellular phones, mobile and wireless computing, video conferencing, and instant credit card verification with the swipe of a plastic card through a machine.

> **"The effects of technology do not occur at the level of opinions or concepts, but alter sense ratios or patterns of perception steadily and without any resistance."**
>
> —MARSHALL MCLUHAN
> *The Medium Is the Message, 1967*

The expanding expectations of choice characteristic of the new consumer are one effect of growing time pressure. To the time-conscious shopper, the most generous possible menu of purchase options offering several different price-points cuts down on time spent driving around hunting and comparison shopping. Category-killing, price-sensitive retail chains like Wal-Mart (www.wal-mart.com) and "warehouse clubs" like Price-Costco (www.wal-pricecostco.com) and Sam's Club (www.samsclub.com) serve the needs of discount-minded and low-income shoppers who want to pile up the largest number of bargains with the smallest outlay of time and effort. Pier 1 Imports (www.pier1.com) actually urges shoppers to take home a piece of rattan furniture or a dhurrie rug and try it out. It wants to encourage would-be buyers put off by not having the time to make the perfect selection and afraid of making a costly mistake. The no-questions-asked, hassle-free policies for exchanging or returning goods pioneered by stores like Nordstrom in the early 1980s are similarly motivated.

Yet even these leaders in serving the new consumer's needs have little cause to relax into smug self-congratulation. Today's consumers are made more aware by modern communications, they have more choice, they are more diverse and mobile; yet the pace of life has also made them more discontented. As a result, the American consumer's demands on the supplier appear, for all the world, to be increasing exponentially.

The New Consumer Is Never a Satisfied Consumer

A 1995 report in *Fortune* (http://pathfinder.com/fortune) set out the results of a customer satisfaction survey by the University of Michigan Business School (www.bus.umich.edu) and the American Society for Quality Control (www.asqc.org). Not even Federal Express—"a service star"—earned a rating above 85 on a scale of 0 to 100. (Although Dole Foods, purveyor of pineapple rings and other packaged consumables, did earn a top score of 90. See www.dole5aday.com.) According to the report:

> *"(I Can't Get No) Satisfaction" is the theme song of consumers who clearly believe the nation's companies are doing a lousy job of meeting their needs....Many of the losers on the list are champs in both size and reputation. Citicorp [www.citicorp.com] has the most advanced ATM system in the world and a global strategy as ambitious as Coca-Cola's [www.cocacola.com]. But consumers find banking there anything but refreshing....Nordstrom [www.nordstrom.com], famous for taking shoppers by the hand, is not the crowd pleaser you might think, either: The department store barely broke 80.*[1]

Companies with the clearest view of the new consumer's time-conscious mental landscape that are willing to adapt their modus operandi to its features will have the edge over their competition.

New consumers expect from organizations if not obeisance then, at the very least, the respect accorded an equal. Traditional business language reveals a different attitude on the part of managers, who have unthinkingly referred to marketing "targets" slotted into market "segments" of people with wants and needs assumed to be virtually identical. Consumers have been thought of in terms of classification statistics—"30–40 age bracket, $70,000–$100,000 income range, 2.5 children, 2.5 cars"—or categories—such as DINKS (dual income, no kids)—to be manipulated into desiring the goods or services a company has to purvey. The general idea has been that if you could name it, classify it, and put it in a database, you had half the marketing problem solved. These practices are symptomatic of an obsession with measurement in the interests of control (over the partitioned groups).

The other half of the misguided marketing equation has dictated that dealing with individual consumers is a waste of time. And time is money. Therefore, the argument goes, it is necessary to classify consumers into large monolithic groups and address them as if they all think and act alike. While this approach may have been expedient in the age of mass marketing, it is unlikely to survive the reign of the new consumer.

A New Model to Fit the New Consumer

The new marketing model reflects a shift from monologue to dialogue in dealings with customers. The result is a reversal of traditional consumer and producer roles, with the consumer dictating exactly how he or she would like to be served. New consumers expect to be asked about their individual preferences and treated—to the most extreme degree possible—as if these preferences are being respected.

A pioneering example of the consultative approach in action is the way Philips Electronics N.V. (www.philips.com), the Dutch multinational giant, developed an on-line product for children in the early 1990s.[2] Philips dispatched industrial designers, cognitive psychologists, anthropologists, and sociologists in mobile vans to communities in Italy, France, and the Netherlands. The researchers invited adults and children to brainstorm ideas for new electronics products. Instead of conducting a survey of these volunteer product designers, Philips arranged discussions in which specialists and customers imagined new possibilities. After examining all the propositions the dialogues produced, Philips reduced them to a short list, then chose one new interactive product. In the next stage, the researchers revisited the communities and tested the new product idea on the same children whose aid had been enlisted.

The gains to be had from consulting consumers in this fashion are also demonstrated by a progressive Parisian designer of women's clothes, Emanuel Ungaro, which licenses a line of garments to Gruppo GFT, which in turn distributes them in America. The "relaxed career wear" bearing the Emanuel label has been one of the few upscale collections in the business to thrive in a shrinking market, the result of an apparent decline in women's interest in high-fashion clothing. Analyzing Emanuel's success in a report on the garment industry, the *New York Times* said in 1996:

> In fashion, manufacturers usually rely on intuition and on feedback from retailers. Instead, Emanuel executives went right to customers, in suburbs as well as cities. "We're doing a lot more analysis today than we did in the past because now the customer wants to tell the designer what she wants," said Maura de Vischier, chief executive of Emanuel.[3]

> **In the real time corporation, customers are treated like partners.**

TQM (described in the introduction to this book) supplies the model. Enlightened companies invite customers to sit on advisory boards, work as partners in the refinement of specifications and testing, share benchmark data, and fine-tune the balance of supply and demand. Customers have an equal say in such areas as design and inventory management. Customers—like vendors—are treated like partners.

Caution: Slow-Moving Vehicles Ahead

In addition to such exemplary exercises in paying attention to market feedback as displayed by Philips and Emanuel, recent history supplies cautionary tales about companies taking the opposite tack. German automaker Porsche (www.porsche.be), for instance, lost 80 percent of its share of the American luxury car market to Japanese rivals in just five years in the late 1980s and early 1990s. Until the company ran into trouble, it refused to lower its prices—even over a period in which the dollar lost more than half its value against the mark.[4]

Both Porsche and Mercedes (www.daimler-benz.com) mistakenly believed that the appeal of brand exclusivity—and in the case of Mercedes, outstanding engineering—gave them license to price as they pleased. In 1990 I attended a J. D. Power conference at which the keynote address was delivered by the director of marketing for Mercedes America. He boasted that while other automakers were lowering prices and so devaluing their brands, Mercedes would soon announce even more expensive models. Only a few months later, Lexus appeared on the scene, forcing Mercedes to modify its pricing and change many of its other entrenched marketing practices. But a great deal of damage had been done. Daimler-Benz lost almost $4 billion in 1995.

In Porsche's case, large portions of its potential market, in which baby boomers were heavily represented, were starting families and rapidly switching from deluxe cars to minivans or buying the smart new Lexus. In addition, the government slapped on new luxury sales and gas taxes, and the economy was in a recession. Finally, with Porsche in the red and its unit sales dropping steeply, the company, like Mercedes, was sufficiently humbled to introduce new cars with more modest tags. The result was a dramatic increase in sales by 1997. Porsche's slow response was almost catastrophic and its market share growth much slower. Brand name was no protection.

Companies poorly oriented to the technology-toned consumer's changing behavioral terrain often describe their preferences in clever-sounding terms derived from interpretations of research rather than interactive information. But the properly oriented company will set itself the goal of understanding the consumer through dialogue. It knows that customers bombarded with sales propositions that do not reflect responsiveness to their needs will increasingly react with Procrustean fury or, worse, fatal indifference.

Real time marketing permits the constant updating of information about consumers' likes and dislikes; communications and computer technologies are now closely meshed for a constant exchange of information between distributors, retailers, and customers. Networks of this sort already exist and register rapidly changing consumer wishes. Computer-based design and manufacturing technologies are allowing companies to go even further, actually responding to those wishes with fiercely compressed product cycles and processes that incorporate more options and variety.

Virtual Customization through Service

The fact is, now that the technological means for enormous flexibility exist, what customers expect is customization or personalization of some kind. The costs of customizing manufactured goods are falling steadily as technical refinements and managerial innovations allow flexible production plants with short runs to get closer to the low unit costs of long mass production runs. Undifferentiated manufactured goods are a steadily diminishing proportion of the output of advanced economies.

Manufacturers like Levi Strauss (www.levi.com) have been lighting the way to the future: since 1995, Levi's sales clerks have taken the measurements of women shopping for jeans and entered the numbers into computers that calculate fit. The customized jeans are sewn at a Levi's factory from a computer-generated pattern. A shoe-store chain, the Custom Foot, (www.thecustomfoot.com) lets women design their own shoes, using a three-dimensional foot scanner.[5] Variety, when it is broad enough, can amount to virtual customization—whether in the form of products actually sitting on retail shelves or capable of being ordered directly from the factory in a quantity of one.

From the consumer's viewpoint, individual attention also amounts to virtual customization. For instance, though doctors and lawyers usually draw on the same database of knowledge—a combination of their training and experience—to serve patients or clients, they apply that knowledge to specific clients in specific ways, tailored to individual needs. Every ulcer patient may be prescribed the same drug and dietary regimen, but feels as if he or she has received customized attention.

Unfortunately, health care today is being driven by health care maintenance organizations (HMOs), which are degrading patient care to a one-prescription-fits-all commodity business. Consumers are becoming increasingly dissatisfied with the severe constraints on choice of physicians, cumbersome proce-dures for treatment approval, endless paperwork, and red tape associated with their health insurance. This approach to service will eventually fail because it violates the basic tenets of good service: interaction, a willingness to listen on the part of the ser-vice provider, customized responsiveness, and real time.

Real time technology holds the potential for restoring sub-stance and meaning to the care in health care. I have been a dia-betic for more than forty years. In that span of time, I have been able to take advantage of specialized new products and medical technologies—everything from a huge and growing range of sugar-free foods to pen-size, thirty-second test glucose monitors to a miniature pump that acts as an electronic pancreas supplying insulin twenty-four hours a day, whenever and wherever I need it. I frequently correspond via e-mail with my doctor, Joe Prendergast,. A practicing diabetologist for more than twenty-five years, he runs the Endocrine Metabolic Medical Centre (EMMC) in Atherton, California (www.diabeteswell.com).

EMMC is a model of futuristic responsiveness in health care. Its operation is guided by the findings of the Diabetic Control and Complications Trial, released in 1993. This study showed that any improvement in blood glucose control reduced the risk of the various complications associated with the disease. EMMC has been conducting an experiment with Caresoft, a Silicon Valley startup (www.caresite.com), to help a subset of its patients who are having trouble maintaining their blood glucose levels within desired ranges and happen to be connected to the Internet. Caresoft has developed "condition management" software that enables clinic staff to assist such patients, directly and proactively, over the Internet in a secure environment. "Data are the key to control," says Dr. Prendergast. Hence diabetics upload data from their digital glucose monitoring devices and transmit these to the care givers, and in return they get recommendations and reminders from the system, and instant feedback on actions to take from the care giver.

While the number of patients in this pilot project is small, preliminary results show a marked improvement in their ability to control their ailment. "Patient empowerment," Dr. Prendergast believes, is " probably the most philosophically exciting idea to emerge in medicine in recent years." He is trying to extend many of his findings about the effectiveness of patient power to a wider public through an organization he founded, the Pacific Medical Research Foundation. Empowerment is inextricably linked to customization.

Technology-toned consumers do not merely want a customized end product. They also require some sign that a company acknowledges their individuality in almost all of its dealings with them. Personalized greetings at a hotel—"Welcome back, Mr. McKenna, thanks for staying with us. Your favorite room is available for you"—are not the half of it. I didn't realize what heights my own expectations had reached until a remark I made to a shirt salesman earned a look of horror from my wife. "We sell lots of these," he said, pressing one selection on me. "Now why would I want to wear a shirt that everyone else is wearing?" I snapped at him reflexively.

A similarly harsh and thoroughly contemporary attitude is expressed in the *New York Times* report on the garment industry, mentioned above:

> *Walk through the Macy's in Herald Square and experience the world of a lab mouse. Go to the contemporary department, home to shiny sheath dresses and polyester hip huggers, and realize that a coat to wear over them means a trip to another floor. Like that suit and want a nice scarf to wear with it? Trek downstairs to accessories. Over at coats, an indifferent sales clerk, punching sales tags into the computer with all the enthusiasm of a child being immunized, should not be asked to recommend a nice pair of matching boots. They will be nowhere nearby.*[6]

QUESTIONS OR COMMENTS ABOUT THIS PRODUCT CALL TOLL-FREE WEEKDAYS 9-4 EST. 1-800-468-1714.

New customers want to feel that they have the ear of employees with the authority to make swift decisions and, increasingly, that they can reach someone who can take action. The most progressive companies allow customers access to huge corporate product-related and service databases. Today, an 800 number is even printed on a package of M&M's (1-800-627-7852) and a bar of Hershey's chocolate (1-800-468-1714). Some companies have already taken the step of printing the address of their Web site on their products (Pepsi is an example: www.pepsi.com), thereby providing the consumer with a gateway to galaxies of information. Information provided at a hypothetical M&M's site, for instance, could range from a graphical demonstration or video of how the candy is manufactured to research information about the profiles of people who prefer eating green M&M's to red ones. Some day a customer with a malfunctioning electric toaster will be able to download diagrams demonstrating troubleshooting procedures—unless she decides to return or exchange the appliance and is instructed as to how to go about this painlessly over the Internet or by fax.

VISIT PEPSI WORLD ON THE INTERNET
http://www.pepsi.com

Making Choice Transparent

Above all, what the new consumers want is control, which chiefly means choice, even if they are not sufficiently conscious of that desire for control (or choice) to be capable of expressing it in a focus group. They want not only the widest array of choices but a choice among choice-making routes.

One route, for instance, would spare people the burden of choosing at all. Someone wanting this option might share the opinion of Natan Sharansky, a member of the Israeli Knesset, who after nine years in Soviet prisons and labor camps complained of feeling lost in the West. Forced to make "thousands of mundane choices [about] all these kinds of orange juice and cereals," he said, "[y]ou lose your life in all these things. Your life becomes very shallow."[7] Precisely that sentiment is echoed at the start of the 1996 film *Trainspotting*, adapted from the novel of the same name, about young, heroin-addicted Scottish dropouts. A voiceover conveys the disgust the main character, Mark Renton, feels over the commercial rituals of modern society:

> *Choose life. Choose a job….Choose a fucking big television, choose washing machines, cars, compact disc players and electrical tin openers….Choose fixed-interest mortgage repayments. Choose a starter home….Choose leisurewear and matching luggage. Choose a three-piece suit…in a range of fucking fabrics….Choose your future. Choose life.*[8]

For Renton, the burden of choice is overwhelming, but there are constructive new alternatives to his drug-induced oblivion. In 1996, Rates Technology of Long Island patented a telecommunications device that can automatically select the cheapest carrier—among all carriers nationwide, a total of 867 at the time—for every long-distance call placed. As soon as a phone number is punched in, the computerized processor scans all the rates of all the carriers before it makes its selection.[9]

Choice ultimately becomes transparent to the user, by virtue of either an easy-to-use interface or simple familiarity. Transparency means never having to say, "Damnit!" When information is available at the touch of a fingertip, you have transparency. Software developed by the Colorado start-up Netdelivery enables publishers of catalogs, newspapers, newsletters, and any sort of material that requires constant updating to be placed on a subscriber's computer automatically without the user phoning, searching, clicking, or downloading. Transparency! Using such software delivers your daily financial newsletter or Lands' End catalog to the desktop—always current, prices, pictures, and all (www.netdelivery.com). The most successful transparent human interface is the simple, twelve-button alphanumeric telephone keypad, which offers an almost infinite choice of communication links—not just to other owners of telephones but to information services and directories—with the user exerting little thought or effort.

For the majority who actually enjoy being offered a choice, the options provided by real time technology will be unprecedented. The person buying a car, probably long before he or she visits a showroom to kick actual tires and take a test drive, will have done these things "virtually," in some sense, through on-line services. The potential buyer will have browsed through comparative data and the Web site of, say, *Consumer Reports* (www.consumer.org); J. D. Power & Associates (www.JDPower.com), the organization that monitors automobile trends and performance; or the Consumer Information Center at www.pueblo.gsa.gov. Nationally distributed car magazines have Web sites, as do brokers stocked with vast reservoirs of data about the relative costs and benefits of purchasing and leasing. There are Internet bulletin boards linking de facto communities of owners of different makes and models of cars, through which additional help and advice can be sought.

> **When information is available without any effort, you have transparency.**

A friend of mine recently purchased a new minivan after using the Internet to gather data and a fax machine to send out requests for bids to dealers. She said it was the "best and most efficient experience I have ever had of buying a car." The automobile business is being reshaped from the bottom up by the discovery of exactly this sort of potential. "The consumer-driven marketplace is changing the heart and soul of this industry," Dave Power, J. D. Power & Associates founder, told me. "The franchise retail system is a hundred years old! Things have to change. The whole system is broken."[10]

Today's leaders—embryonic real time organizations—are already putting in place the managerial and technical infrastructure to give consumers more information and assistance, making choice as easy as possible. They understand the edge this gives them with customers pressured on all fronts: putting in longer work days to stay ahead of the competition or to assuage fears of downsizing; straining to find time to spend with children and equally harassed mates; longing for increasingly scarce leisure time or the time to simply get chores done.

All Information Superhighways Lead to Service

Companies have long competed largely through building brand names—sowing desirable associations in the minds of potential customers with advertising slogans, discounts, and promotions. Customers have been treated like clay to be molded into loyal brand buyers. Today's enlightened company understands that lasting brand loyalty is won only one way: by dynamically *serving* customers. Here *dynamic* means constant interaction and dialogue based on real time information systems.

Real time service is the key to winning the hearts and minds of new consumers, with their seemingly reset circadian clocks. It means being in touch all the time, creating an experience, adding information that addresses individual needs and circumstances, responding without delay, and gaining valuable feedback for new and improved offerings.

Internet enthusiasts eagerly await access to devices that will allow them to be on-line without interruption—or, in the telling phrase they use, "turned on" twenty-four hours a day. Rising businesses aiming to excel in the real time arena have as their goal ubiquitous, nonstop, and transparent service.

The new consumers hate to be kept waiting and are being conditioned, in all spheres of life, to become ever more impatient. "The advances of technology contradict theories of human satisfaction expounded by...psychoanalysis," Nobel Prize–winning novelist Nadine Gordimer observes. "Apart from its purely sexual application, Sigmund Freud's deferred pleasure as a refinement of emotional experience does not compare with the immediate joy of hearing a lover's voice, or getting a friend's reply to a letter at once by e-mail."[11]

As I have noted elsewhere,[12] what customers want most from a product is often qualitative and intangible: it is the benefit and service that is integral to the product. Service is not an event; it is the process of creating a customer environment of information, assurance, and comfort. Technology has made it possible to establish such an environment with unprecedented finesse. Many companies are using call centers, kiosks, 800 numbers, expert software, and on-line services to meld marketing and technology, creating a feedback loop that binds their best interests to those of their customers. This circuit has immensely enhanced sensitivity to customers' requirements and to many of their preoccupations with information and service, most of which have a time-related component.

From its earliest days, the world's leading microprocessor company, Intel, discussed plans for future models of microchips with designer-engineers at customer companies, such as computer makers. As Dave House, a former senior vice president at Intel, explained to me, by blending marketing and engineering, the company has been able to achieve a faster return on investment in new products. Working closely with key customers on

The Twenty-Four-Hour Consumer

Every moment of the day is packed with pleasure and work intermixed. There is a pressing demand for access, conveyance, choice, and real time gadgets because there is "no time."

6:00 A.M.	Awakened by CD music, e-mail monitor, security appliance controller.
6:30 A.M.	Work out with Nautilus, read newspapers on Exercycle.
7:00 A.M.	Go to home office on-line: Answer e-mail, order book, order Lands' End shirt, pay bills-EFT, download newspaper, upgrade software.
7:30 A.M.	Have breakfast: Starbucks, Bagel Shop.
8:30 A.M.	Staff meeting, video conference center.
10:00 A.M.	Attend customer teleconference meeting.
11:00 A.M.	Return voice mail calls from car cellular.
11:30 A.M.	Beeper reminder: Keep appointment at Weight Watchers.
11:45 A.M.	Have fitting for custom jeans and shoes.
Noon	Get lunch at Burger King drive through.
12:30 P.M.	Receive car fax from Lexus dealer: "30,000 mile check-up due."
1:00 P.M.	Board ticketless flight to L.A. Confirm appointments in-flight.
1:30 P.M.	Confirm rental car reservation made by electronic agent in-flight.
2:00 P.M.	Arrive in L.A. Stuck in traffic for two hours. Tune in twenty-four-hour traffic report. Check guidance display for alternate route.

2:30 P.M.	Cellular phone call to broker; buy Intel. Check voice mail.
4:00 P.M.	Play quick tennis game at traveler's health club.
5:00 P.M.	Gourmet dinner: low salt, no sugar, low cholesterol, nonfat, decaf cappuccino. Charge on Visa to get frequent-flyer points.
7:00 P.M.	Go to self-check-in at hotel.
7:30 P.M.	Go on-line. Reply to e-mail and voice mail; surf Internet.
9:00 P.M.	Watch replay highlights of Atlanta Olympics ($5.95). Prepare sales presentation on multimedia PC.
11:00 P.M.	Take two melatonin to get to sleep fast.
11:30 P.M.	Set drapes to open at 6 A.M.

specifications—balancing prototype products' technical capabilities against customers' receptivity to new features and requirements—Intel has developed a remarkable relationship with those customers, who are then primed to use the products they helped design. As with Philips and the children who participated in its brainstorming meetings, or the customers of the fashion design firm Emanuel, the consultees not only help to make salable products but become potential buyers of them.

This sort of intimate dialogue between a company and its customers creates a brand loyalty immeasurably deeper than catchy jingles riding on advertising blitzes ever could. It creates a quasi-symbiotic tie. The new interactive technologies collapse the space between consumer and producer. The extraordinary attentiveness to customers' desires by companies using these tools leads their customers to expect a similar response from other companies.

The galloping expectations of the technology-toned consumer can be expected to gain velocity as an electronic infrastructure allowing intensifying interactivity between producers and customers spreads wider. This is the infrastructure composed of the communication revolution's profusion of linked media. Collectively, these media represent a critical watershed. For businesses and branches of government serving the public, the important media of the past were channels for broadcast. The vital new media, by contrast, are channels of access.

Access media hold the key to satisfying the consumer's runaway demands for real time results. This is because access media help organizations serve customers better by making it possible for customers to serve *themselves*. Without any sense of effort, customers are satisfied by means of sophisticated, hidden, or "transparent" technologies about whose workings they need know nothing.

The real time message:

New consumers are never satisfied consumers. Managers hoping to serve them must work to eliminate time and space constraints on service. They must push the technological bandwidth with interactive dialogue systems—equipped with advanced software interfaces—in the interest of forging more intimate ties with these consumers. Managers must exploit every available means to obtain their end: building self-satisfaction capabilities into services and products and providing customers with access anytime, anywhere.

Automation or cybernation deals with all the units and components of the industrial and marketing process exactly as radio or TV combines the individuals in the audience into new inter-process. The new kind of interrelation in both industry and entertainment is the result of the electric instant speed. Our new electric technology now extends the instant processing of knowledge by

3 What Is the Message When the Medium Is Everywhere?

interrelation that has long occurred within our central nervous system.

—MARSHALL MCLUHAN, *Understanding Media*, 1964

Post-industrial creatures of an information economy, we increasingly sense that accessing media is what we do.

—WILLIAM GIBSON, *New York Times Magazine*, July 14, 1996

MEDIA, PLANETWIDE, are the star attraction of our time. Probably no other class of human-made phenomena so dominates our lives. Their effects on society are older than the revelations of the scribes who wrote the 2,000-year-old Dead Sea Scrolls.

Media: Mimic of Our Human Expressions

As Marshall McLuhan showed us, media are extensions of ourselves. From stone to papyrus and paper to electrons, media carry what we know, how we think, what we dream of and desire, what transactions we conduct. In all their shapes and forms, from television to cyberspace, media are considered by many to be the most effective means of engaging human attention and influencing human behavior.

This is truer today than ever before, even if the newest forms of media have upended the quintessential twentieth-century fear of media as the means for Big Brother to lash society to his ends. Instead, the most novel media could not be more profoundly democratizing in their effects or more destructive of centralized authority, whether in government, religion, health care, education, or—especially, as I demonstrate in this chapter—business. The new media have Big

Brother on the run, a fugitive on a teeming thoroughfare of bits and bytes.

Media and society are developing together, as if in lockstep. *Networking*, significantly, has been gaining currency as both a social and an electronic term. As media acquire bandwidth and expressive range, they exhibit more and more human-like characteristics. Conversely, they allow us to be simultaneously more individualistic and more collaborative; they are helping us to build communities of common and uncommon interests; they are reshaping the social environment.

As with all technologies, the potential of new media can rarely be assessed by looking for clues in places where the conditioning of the past guides judgment and opinion. In the 1980s, when the personal computer was in its early stages of market development, a well-regarded research firm conducted a national social trends survey and predicted that the then-budding industry was in for big trouble. The survey showed that the American people did not want more technology encroaching on their lives. The conclusion drawn was that consumers would resist the notion of a personal computer and that the industry would therefore develop slowly, if at all.

My response to that conclusion was that it was dead wrong—that strangeness rapidly disappears with constant contact with the new and unfamiliar, whether in art, food, science, or technology, which is arguably least intrusive and most transforming when ubiquitous yet hardly visible. Much of it, like the fractional horse power motor, is hidden deep inside appliances and gadgets, with its least interesting—strictly utilitarian—features on display. You might almost say it is in the nature of technology to hide its complexity. In their extreme sensitivity and responsiveness to our particular needs and desires, digital technologies of the future will scarcely seem to be there at all. This genie-like transparency is one of the profound differences between future media and those of the past.

New Media Are Interactive

We have all had a foretaste of the possibilities of new media. A few years ago, an earthquake woke me at one o'clock in the morning in a Tokyo hotel room. As a resident of shake-prone California for decades, I automatically reached for the remote control and turned on the TV set, assuming that if I saw announcers interrupting programming and frantically running for cover, I would have to abandon my hotel. But after some channel surfing, I found all the Japanese transmissions serenely undisturbed. Then I got CNN (www.cnn.com). Within seconds, the program in process was interrupted for a report of a 4.5 tremor—background graphics showed concentric circles with Tokyo at the center—broadcast from a studio in Atlanta, Georgia. A CNN reporter in Tokyo, jolted awake like me, had called his news desk in Atlanta, which in turn had called the closest geological station and got the Richter reading (www.neic.cr.usgs.gov).

Time and space are transformed by real time information technology.

It had taken me a scant few minutes to confirm what I suspected had happened miles beneath Japan with a source halfway around the world. I had had a McLuhanesque experience of the most dramatic sort—that is, an experience of media in the broadest possible sense of the term, as extensions of our ability to see and hear and touch, extensions of the human nervous system. I had taken for granted the innumerable connections involved, between technological devices and organizations, to tell me what I wanted to know—on the one hand, the TV set, the satellite dish and decoder, the satellite uplinks and downlinks; on the other, the hotel, the Japanese cable company, the Intelsat, and, finally, CNN. All of the conduits and joints en route had been "transparent" to me, a transparency that partly accounts for television's subtle, quasi-subliminal conditioning of its audiences.

The newest media—creations of microprocessors, bits, bytes per second, the Internet, and satellite technology—are by far the most formidable agents of conditioning behind the culture of acceleration reshaping the marketplace. In addition to transparency and speed, two distinguishing features account for their extraordinary power to transform: First, interactivity. Second, entertainment—or the use of human "interfaces" of the most affecting sort, borrowing techniques from the entertainment business.

Interactive media give consumers control and unprecedented influence over what companies offer them, as well as when and where they do so. To return for a moment to my experience of an earth tremor in Tokyo: With an interactive device of the decade ahead, my TV would also have become a direct link to Tokyo's twenty-four-hour Earthquake Information Center (Japan has one of the most sophisticated earthquake monitoring and research activities in the world [www.eri.utokyo. ac.jp]). I might have selected English from a menu of languages, then pointed at my location on a city map and received instant information and emergency instructions, if necessary. Instead of being at the mercy of filtered and delayed broadcast information, I would have had the immediate experience and comfort of information *access*, helping myself to precisely what I wanted to know, virtually in real time.

We commonly think of media as *the* media, meaning video and print communication channels—television, newspapers, or magazines—rather than as what they actually are, the plural form of *medium*, or a means of conveyance. Traditional broadcast media can be seen as one-way pipes. The new forms of interactive digital media are bidirectional. They come in a variety of forms and can be embedded inside almost anything, from kiosks to kitchen appliances. After this evolutionary shift, mass (broadcast) media as we know them today will be virtually unrecognizable. Digital media increasingly bring the user under the spell of conveyance and facility. They transform behavior by giving people unprecedented access to all kinds of places, people, and ideas unconstrained by time, culture, or geography. Consumers are being taught by these media to unlearn their conditioning by repetitious broadcast messages.

As Nicholas Negroponte, founder of the Media Lab at the Massachusetts Institute of Technology (www.media.mit.edu), puts it in his book *Being Digital*,

> *Being digital will change the nature of mass media from a process of pushing bits at people to one of allowing people (or their computers) to pull at them.*[1]

Just as fast and easy-to-use ATMs have become a part of daily life, many other transactions will turn transparent—that is, become streamlined and unobtrusive: We'll make airline, car rental, and hotel reservations ourselves without human intermediaries; have medical lab work done at the local pharmacy; buy and sell stocks anytime, anyplace; hold three-way parent-teacher-student conferences on-line; and broadcast amateur comedy shows from our living rooms.

Deborah Doyle McWhinney, Visa International (www.VISA.com)

ATM networks are embryonic real time systems, and Deborah Doyle McWhinney, executive vice president at Visa International, is a pioneer in their design, installation, and management. She talked with me about what this experience has taught her about the technology-toned consumer.

I have been able to observe—and in some cases drive—fundamental changes in consumer banking behavior. Managing the Consumer Electronic Banking Division for Bank of America [www.bankamerica.com], I led a team that helped to build the largest ATM network in the world. It was kind of a push-pull affair, in terms of us trying to get our customers to use the ATMs. In the early days, we were largely pushing the consumer to use the ATMs for routine banking transactions—for example, cash withdrawals, deposits, transfers, payments, and balance inquiries. Then, as the Versateller ATM service began to mature, what we discovered was, customers were actually happier with the automated, self-service mode. I watched it for many years, and I really think what happened was that customer usage of ATMs—and the level of customers' expectations—entered kind of a spiral, just went up and up.

The customers who chose to do business with us were the ones to whom time and choice were important commodities. No longer were these customers constrained by "banker's hours." They could deposit their payroll check when they got off the plane or on their way from the daycare center.

Bank of America's customers today use the ATMs for deposits at record levels, and I think it was because, many years ago, senior management allowed me to give preferential treatment to ATM deposits throughout the system—cut-off times were later. Basically, we didn't put all the checks and deposits coming into those accounts on hold, because it meant better customer service.

As other self-service tools were introduced, such as voice-response telephone service, we found the acceptance curve far steeper than we had assumed. Again, customers liked the choice. Our differentiating strategy began to take on a life of its own. Customers were now pulling us to improve the service in new ways. Service availability twenty-four hours a day, seven days a week was a must. If the Versateller ATM network went down, the outage was discussed on the morning or evening commute news. ATMs became a way of life.

The bank moved aggressively into allowing customers to use

their Versatel card at the point of sale—to buy groceries and gas. Then the bank added the Visa logo to the ATM card, so most customers could use their card in lieu of a check to make purchases at virtually any merchant in the world. And, again, the rate of acceptance was better than we expected.

Up to 1994, for probably three or four years, I had been able to predict what the ATM usage numbers at Bank of America would be—all the way from 47 percent of our customers, until it got to 60 percent. Then, all of a sudden, last year, we did a big push to get customers to use electronic funds transfer—deposits for Social Security checks and payroll checks. We thought we might get, like, 100,000 customers to do this. Instead, we got half a million. This April I made a prediction that in December we'd have more deposits going through the ATMs than in the branches, but it happened two months later! Now you could say, well, what difference does six months make? But I really think that you've hit a nerve here, with your ideas about real time. I think that there's a new curve emerging in consumer behavior: the adoption of electronics and of these on-line types of services gains critical mass faster than in the past, and happens much more broadly.

Look at the Internet. While it has been around for a long time, access has only been generally available for the last twenty-four months. Already the acceptance is astounding. I believe it took ATMs almost fifteen years to reach the same usage levels that Internet services did in two years. Just think of the implications!

Successful organizations are going to find that the service model consumers want is really *choice when they want it, on the terms they want*. The idea of self-service, in the early days, had a negative connotation, like pumping your own gas and things like that, but now it amounts to service with choice. Maybe we should come up with a new name for self-service!

Today's consumer is very savvy. Consumers understand the value chain. If they serve themselves, they understand what savings that means to the company. They will expect to share in some of the savings in terms of price breaks or other incentives. On the other hand, if they want the full-service, red carpet treatment, someone holding their hand through the whole transaction, they expect that it will cost more.

The customers we are dealing with today are much more logical about how business is done. From choosing banks to hotels, they know that the more extras they want, the more they will pay. That is a very important paradigm for those of us involved in the development of electronic commerce to consider. I would imagine that we're going to start seeing companies with really famous service, like Nordstrom, Nike, Disney, reassessing how they do what they do, based on these kinds of considerations.

New Media Will Transform Business

Access media are spurring a reimagining and redesign of almost every familiar and ordinary human activity. Interactivity is coming into play everywhere in business—wherever organizations perceive opportunities to better serve their customers by giving them access to means of serving themselves. The tools already exist for businesses to create their own channels, networks, and programming for dialogue with or "narrowcasting" to employees and customers.

In February 1994, Hyatt Hotels & Resorts (www.hyatt.com) began to offer guests at some of its branches the use of an electronic check-in and check-out kiosk located in the lobby. Checking in, guests with reservations run their credit cards through a slot in the kiosk, then touch a screen to choose between rooms for smokers and nonsmokers, with or without views, and so on. Next, the kiosk returns a key card and a folder imprinted with the selected room number. At check-out time, the kiosk spits out an itemized list of charges. That same check-in, check-out hotel kiosk could be a communications channel for making rental car or airplane reservations, checking on the weather in another city, obtaining stock market quotes, sending an e-mail message, or watching a two-minute entertainment video clip.

But that's not all. Just as we have seen TV viewing channels multiply, so will corporate channels and networks. Company communication channels will be developed so that corporations can interact not just with customers but also with the broad spectrum of their stakeholders. Business-to-business networks may become an ever-present educational resource, showing organizations how to refine their offerings for greater appeal to buyers.

As judged by the standards of the past, all the new and incipient forms of dialogue represent a radical shift in approach, a change the enormity of which I remind myself with an incident that dates to the mid-1960s, when I bought a defective RCA television set. Tired of the local RCA dealer's inadequate explanations for the cause of the trouble and weeks of procrastination for repairs, I called the head of the company's consumer products division and talked my way past his telephone sentries to get him on the line. I introduced myself and gave him a concise account of my difficulties. In response, he had only one question for me, asked in a tone of icy outrage: "How did you get through?" His reply now seems to me the perfect emblem of companies' attitudes toward customers in the industrial age of marketing.

The real time organization is available to the customer all the time.

Not only is direct access for customers the essence of marketing today, but the organizations most deeply committed to the new model aim to be, in some sense, "with" their customers all the time.

Real Time Communication

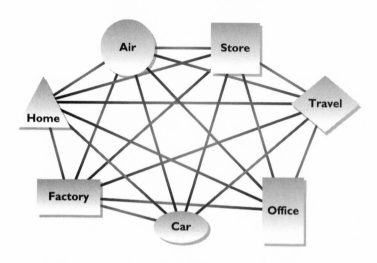

Everything is connected in a vast network. I can do my banking from a car, a grocery store, an office cafeteria, or even a plane. All I need is a connection. Over the next decade, costs of communications will decrease and bandwith will increase, offering more fully human interaction.

Twenty-Four-Hour Bits-Based Dialogue

PepsiCo (www.pepsico.com) supplies an excellent illustration of the shades of interactivity to come. In the summer of 1996, the company offered the young consumers of its Mountain Dew soft drink electronic beepers ordinarily priced at around $60 for $29.99, plus shipping and handling, plus six months of free air time worth $135. For the six months of the promotion, Mountain Dew paged the 50,000 teenage and Generation X participants once a week and gave them a toll-free number to call. Over the telephone connection, these young people could listen to interviews with heroes of so-called extreme sports, such as bungee jumping and sky surfing, that feature in Mountain Dew's TV commercials. They could also learn about opportunities to win discounts and prizes from twenty companies whose buyers overlap heavily with Mountain Dew's so-called "Dew Dudes." These included Burton Snowboards (www.burton.com), Killer Loop sunglasses (www.killerloop.com), Sony Music (www.sony.com), Doritos (www.fritolay.com), Universal Studios (www.univstudios.com), *Spin* magazine (www.enews.com/maga zines/spin), Wave Sport, and K-2 In-Line Skates (www.k2 sports.com). All the brand names on the list had been chosen by Mountain Dew customers in marketing focus groups as companies they would like to hear from.

The idea, as a Mountain Dew marketing director explains, was to offer customers a product to "fit their lifestyle" and make them part of "a really cool network."[2] Not only did the beepers give Mountain Dew access to a segment of the consumer marketplace exceedingly difficult to reach through conventional media—print, radio, and TV advertising as well as telemarketing—but the PepsiCo marketing managers envisaged using the beepers in the future to ask customers their opinions of the product and its advertising and of possible promotions and product ideas. They foresaw interactive communications initiated with beepers—combined with responses and suggestions made at the PepsiCo Web site on the Internet—creating an enormous, nonstop, electronic focus group at a remarkably low cost.

Although this approach to marketing is unproven, it is a foreshadowing of future strategies.

Old Sources of Revenue Will Be Choked Off

Pepsi's sort of dialogue, fostered by the new interactive technologies, will sound the death knell for traditional "informational advertising"—the want ads, radio and TV program schedules, stock and real estate listings—on which newspapers depend for both revenues and readers. Much of the infrastructure for an interactive classified network is already in place. Across the Net, thousands of companies now list job openings on their homepage and servers. The network instantly matches job seekers' qualifications to those openings, supplying a list of possible employment opportunities. Anyone who wants to know more about a particular company can, at the click of a mouse button, browse through financials, product descriptions, benefits, video clips of employees discussing the work environment, and a message from the president. All that is left for the job seeker to do is submit an electronic application. In the future, a unique address number might be assigned to each job seeker, to which she might have former employers and associates e-mail references. Job applicants might be able to call up their files to check on the status of their applications at any time.

Many newspaper publishers today mistakenly believe that the new media are simply about moving classified advertising on-line. In fact, they represent a discontinuous leap in the structure of commerce.

Conventional real estate listings face the same fate as traditional job advertisements. Since 1996, the nationwide real estate franchise chain HFS, Inc., which owns Century 21 Real Estate (www.c21realty.com), among other agencies, has been developing a Web-based listing service for property buyers. Instead of combing through pages of classified ads—a form of "broadcast" information—to find houses in their price range with the features they want, house hunters would type into their computers the names of cities and neighborhoods that interest them, along with their target price range, to get background information. This would include facts about schools and other community facilities, trends in real estate values, as well as photographs and detailed descriptions of houses that fit their budget. In this way, people could search for a house by day or night from anywhere they have access to a computer with an Internet connection. Incidentally, HFS's plan would also help the company attain its goal of cutting down the average number of houses real estate agents show clients from twelve to eight.[3]

Television commercials will hardly be immune from these forces of change. Ed Artzt, chairman and CEO of Procter & Gamble, shocked the advertising community when he addressed the American Association of Advertising Agencies in May 1994. Artzt said:

From where we stand today, we can't be sure that ad-supported TV programming will have a future in the world being created—a world of video on demand, pay per view, and subscription television. Within the next few years—surely before the end of the decade—consumers will be choosing among hundreds of shows and pay-per-view movies. They'll have dozens of home shopping channels. They'll play hours of interactive video games. And for many of these—maybe most—no advertising at all. If that happens, if advertising is no longer needed to pay most of the cost of home entertainment, then advertisers like us will have a hard time achieving the reach and frequency we need to support our brands.[4]

Mass media reflect the technology-induced fragmentation of mass markets. The very essence of the new technological capabilities is to permit business to cater to far narrower segments of society than was ever economically possible with the old tools of mass production.

When everything we encounter is, in some form, interactive information, communication, or entertainment, the role of fixed and static forms of media in our lives will steadily diminish. Which is not to say that newspapers and other traditional media will vanish anytime soon. I believe they will for some years continue to repeat their recent history of upheavals in operations, content, marketing, and ownership. Not one of the big three networks—ABC (www.abc.com), NBC (www.nbc.com), or CBS (www.cbs.com)—remains independent. Though they have retained their names, their ownership and business models have significantly changed, thanks to the growth of cable television and narrowcasting.

Everything Is Entertainment

The new paradigm that PepsiCo's Mountain Dew promotion illustrates—marketing as real time dialogue—also demonstrates the other key facet of the all-pervasive new media: its entertainment value. Human interfaces for sophisticated and (to most people) incomprehensible new technologies beguile and seduce by employing tools drawn from the movies, TV sitcoms, and popular music. It has already become a cliché to say that from education to health care, politics to business, everything is, in some sense, a form of entertainment.

In a 1996 Nielsen Media Research (www.nielsen.com) survey of households with Internet access, 51 percent of respondents gave entertainment as their reason for using the Net; this was followed by those who used it to look up news and current events (49 percent), to investigate computer products (41 percent), to get travel information (30 percent), and to get financial information (26 percent).

In three very different ways, entertainment, more than anything else, is driving the dissemination of the technologies behind the new media, even as it lends them the power to stir and play on human feelings and emotions. First, the new media—because of their novelty and strangeness—are intrinsically entertaining to the more adventurous segments of the population (known as early adopters). Second, though the excitement of exchanging e-mail and searching the Web for their own sake wears off, the expanding bandwidth will offer new forms of information combining voice, video, graphics, e-mail, and video feedback. Finally, entertainment is engagement. It attracts and holds attention.

British commentator Anthony Smith, observing the twentieth century's search for escapist devices, notes that

> [E]ntertainment is crucial to the forms that [these devices] will take and the uses to which they will be put. Entertainment reflects something of the psychic drives that lie deeper than the immediately apparent demands of the market....Ingenuity in the provision of new forms of entertainment is likely to provide much of the drive for big technological leaps.[5]

Only about 30 percent of American homes today have personal computers, while more than 90 percent have TV sets. The creation of a communications infrastructure merging telephone, interactive (cable) television, and personal computing linked to the Internet is being driven, above all, by the certainty of a huge market for movies on demand, home shopping, and other forms of entertainment.

Outlining his plan for maintaining Citibank's lead in upscale consumer banking in Asia, the company's branch banking chief, William Campbell, mentioned adding new languages to the thirteen now handled by Citibank's automatic tellers. He also wants to extend stock-trading and bill-paying capabilities to ATMs. But overall, Campbell's strategy rests on making Citibank viscerally compelling. "I don't think many people feel about their bank the way they feel about Disneyland," he told the *New York Times*.[6] To this end, in Kuala Lumpur, Malaysia, for instance, Citibank ingeniously pampers customers with more than $120,000 in their accounts, giving them access to an exclusive "Citigold" program. They are served tea in a fantasy setting like something from a club in the days of the British Raj. The bank branch has a chandelier, a fountain, and luxurious lounge furniture (www.citibank.com).

Banks once sought images of dignity, reserve, and gray-suited remoteness. Today they seek the peerless skills of the Disney empire to lift people out of dreary daily preoccupations.

Perhaps we will all some day live *inside* entertainment—artifacts of fantasy and distraction. A *New Yorker* profile of a planned community, expected by its writer, social critic Witold Rybczynski, to be a model for the future, featured Celebration, a futuristic town built by the Walt Disney Company (www.disney.com).[7] Celebration is in Florida, on the same 28,000-acre tract of land as the theme park EPCOT. It finally brings to life Walt Disney's original vision for the place, buried in the acronym, which stands for Experimental Prototype Community of Tomorrow. Because Disney conceived of a world in which science and technology would solve nearly all problems, the town has a high-tech infrastructure hidden behind the melange of nostalgic architectural styles—Coastal, Classical, Victorian, Colonial Revival, Mediterranean, and French—in which its houses are being built. Part of Celebration was opened in 1996. Future additions to the town include fiberoptic links between individual homes and the school and between homes and the "health campus." Rybczynski observes,

> The notion that Disney World could be a setting for real life will strike most people as improbable.

Actually, in what cyberpunk fiction writer William Gibson calls our "hypermediated world," the idea seems less preposterous every day. There are all sorts of intriguing testimonials to entertainment's expanding role in framing our existence. After much anxious debate on the matter, some old order Amish communities that had forbidden their members to drive cars and ride motorcycles or even bicycles began to permit the use of in-line skates in the mid-1990s. The preservation of the Amish's austere and traditional way of life is the raison d'être of Amish settlements, and some community elders viewed in-line skates as a serious potential threat to that way of life. Why? Because attached to the skates are three defining features of modernity: speed, convenience, and entertainment.[8]

Society Loves Media, Society Hates Media

Businesses seeking to take advantage of the new media's speed, transparency, interactivity, and ability to engage customers so profoundly will forget at their peril that its power is a double-edged sword. As much as media are perceived to be uncannily pervasive and affecting, they are also perceived as insidious. Many people feel overwhelmed by broadcast media. Many are far more anxious over than delighted by the idea of 500 different television channels. We all have an inborn sense of unease with rapid change, and our uneasiness about the effects of proliferating media—millions of blurred events bombarding our minds each day, changing attitudes, opinions, and behavior—is bound up with our having been cast adrift from our once secure sense of time and place. Many fear that information and media, cloaked in entertainment, could be used—or are being used—to control and manipulate people and society.

In "Buried Alive," film critic David Denby's anguished essay about trying to protect his children from the media onslaught, the author finds himself supporting the advent of the V-chip—the microprocessor to be included in all new TV sets from 1998 on, allowing parents to block out programming they wish to screen from their children—in spite of his passionate advocacy of freedom of expression. This freedom, he reluctantly admits, licenses as much schlock as it does high art. Like himself, he says, many parents are "upset by the way pop culture in all its forms has invaded their homes, and the habits, manners and souls of their children....We all believe in 'choice,' but our children, to our chagrin, may no longer have the choice *not* to live in pop....They are shaped by the media as consumers before they've had a chance to develop their souls."[9]

Tread Carefully, Volatile Reactions Ahead

Managers must constantly be aware of how fine a line separates the impression that companies are using the new media to better understand and serve consumers from the perception that they are trying to exploit customers. PepsiCo, for example, ran into a firestorm of unanticipated criticism with its futuristic promotion involving pagers. The company had assumed that this, of all communications technologies, would be irresistible to parents—helping two-career couples worried about their children's whereabouts to keep in touch with them. Instead, the promotion was denounced as disturbingly manipulative by parents and children's advocates—like the Center for Media Advocacy in Washington, D.C., a watchdog group, and Action for Children's Television.

Concerns about the media's exploitative potential are equaled or exceeded by other fears: of social fragmentation and social polarization; of information (and disinformation) overload; of people disengaged from communal life and ensconced in dream worlds conjured by the technologies of virtual reality. Many people are deeply disturbed by the unresolved questions the new media are raising, some examples of which follow.

Is virtual reality a plus or minus for society, given that it can isolate people in artificial cloisters?

To be sure, virtual reality is not the same as "being there," just as on-line communication lacks the complexity and subtle cues of real life encounters. For important human interactions, nothing is as good as face-to-face contact—or all we can observe or intuit from gestures, body language, tone of voice, facial expression, and a handshake—to decide issues of trust and confidence. On the other hand, the new communications tools allow profoundly human exchanges that would not have been possible before. For example, children seriously or terminally ill in hospitals across the country are being helped to overcome fear and feelings of acute anxiety with the aid of interactive technology and entertainment—everything from simulation to video conferencing is being used to create "virtual playgrounds." I watched one small boy at the (Stanford) Lucile Salter Packard Children's Hospital (www-med.stanford.edu/lpch) get a much-needed break from his ordeal, completely absorbed in a computer game. Using his avatar to execute a move that involved opening a virtual door on his computer screen at the same instant that his friend—a boy his age in a hospital in Pittsburgh—made a matching move, he was lost in the pleasures of the virtual world, enjoyment heightened by long-distance collaboration. That link was created by Starbright Pediatric Network, an affiliation of top medical professionals, technologists, and entertainment specialists that is researching in its Digital Distraction Lab the role that virtual reality software can play in helping seriously ill children better cope with their plight (www.starbright.org).

I use this example to illustrate an optimistic viewpoint of this new media as collaborative, engaging, and certainly a new way of expressing oneself. Stephan Pachikov, founder of the virtual reality software company ParaGraph International (www.paragraph.com), uses the term *alter ego* to describe the personality assumed by the avatar. The avatar's sponsor (the real person) is able to imbue his representative character (the avatar or virtual person) with as much or as little of himself as desired. Through dialogue, shared exploration, and discovery with participating virtual people, the avatar grows in knowledge of "self" and "other." In this way, the collaborating avatars share experiences and "get to know" one another. We may well be witnessing and participating in the evolution of an entirely new form of human communication.

How can anyone create a coherent worldview from the atomization of life experience conveyed by media new and old? How are we to distinguish the real from the unreal, truth from lies, when digital information is so easily manipulated, when we are all but deafened by the cacophony of voices competing for our attention, and when both facts and interpretations of facts are so prolific?

Many an inner-city student, for instance, is faced with the challenge of reconciling the following dissonant perspectives and milieus: television's made-up worlds of both violence and privilege; the orderly universe evoked by computers; a safe community of on-line correspondents; the outer reality of a neighborhood wracked by crime, drugs, and violence. For some of these young people, the challenge may not be surmountable: their actions and the course of their lives will reflect the chaos of their worldview.

On the other hand, the new media will also lay at these students' feet unprecedented opportunities for education, which will hone their critical faculties—a boon, now that we are all obliged to be more self-reliant, with so few ready-made answers in a world of all but defunct authorities: Big Government, Big Business, and Brand Names. New educational facilities created by the new media will shatter the old molds.

The new media will supply new means of discriminating between what is real and unreal, true and false. Close, triangulated collaboration between teachers, students, and parents, for example, will become easy over the Internet. Ideally, educational on-line services will encourage teachers to modify curricula for their individual students, not just for particular classes. Parents will be able to "sit in" on electronic classes and get lesson plans customized for their children. Though on-line educational facilities will neither make books obsolete nor serve as adequate substitutes for the attention of gifted teachers, they will stimulate new relationships—not just between students and teachers and parents but with, for instance, experts in domains of specialized knowledge who typically have no time to visit one of today's traditional classrooms or are simply too far away for this to be possible.

The new media will give everyone, not just students, the ready means for feedback, questions, demands, and the ability to seek out views different from any that are doled out to us or that we get by means of force feeding. Unfortunately, this does not mean truth will be any easier to arrive at. We will just have more tools with which to explore and debate the issues. We can hope that the consequences of all this will be increased human communication, interaction, and understanding.

How do we avoid the numbing of our emotions in the media assault?

Immersed in media, it is all too easy to become emotionally alienated. People like myself sat in comfortable living rooms watching snipers in real time on the streets of Sarajevo. Confronted with the horror of what we were witnessing, we hit the psychological equivalent of a remote control button to switch off emotionally, telling ourselves—at some unconscious level—that it was only virtual reality. Yet in other ways, the new media can foster empathy and cultural integration, sometimes across vast geographical distances. One student in Germany and another in the United States, 8,000 miles apart, can converse on-line in real time, in school or at home. As they sharpen their language skills, they can strike up a friendship and benefit incalculably from exposure to another culture, to other ways of thinking and doing. On a wider scale, there seems ample room for optimism about the prospect of a crumbling of phobic walls of prejudice based on color, religion, sex, and class.

In general, insofar as multimedia bind people together in constant dialogue, we can envision that the new media will allow immeasurably more emotional and intellectual engagement than traditional media have. The old media have long made promises they cannot keep, presenting, as they do, hopes and visions without listening to the feedback of the hopeless. Like the other technologies of the twentieth century, they have been largely useless in addressing the fundamental problems of poverty, war, and prejudice. At the very least, the new media allow everyone to tell his or her story. I am not so foolish as to believe that new technology can solve all of society's problems. But it seems to me that we have nothing to lose by making a grab for all the new potential that dialogue and networks offer in the twenty-first century.

Good-Bye Consumer Marketing: Welcome to the Crossroads of the Electronic Market

Of course, technology itself is ideologically neutral. Electrons bear no allegiance to anyone or anything, nor does the Internet, the quintessential access medium. From the perspective of business, by the end of the 1990s, when there could—by some estimates—be 200 million Internet users in America, this medium will most closely resemble an ancient marketplace on the Silk Route (http://ess1.ps.usi.edu~oliver/silk.html). These bazaars did not serve merely for the exchange of goods. They were a cultural crossroads where people swapped stories, news, and traditions. Merchants, philosophers, spies, mountebanks, pamphleteers, and prophets plied their trades.

All of that cheerful chaos will be reproduced on-line. Companies will schmooze with customers, prospective customers, and other companies; customers with other customers. Electronic "personal agent" software—specialized in scouting the Web to retrieve information serving the particular needs and interests of particular users—will dive into catalogs, corporate databases, stock market reports, publishers' backlists, and product data, executing transactions while their users sleep. Already, many senior managers enthusiastically tell me how they spend an hour or two on the Internet every evening, keeping up on the activities of competitors and suppliers, reading university research papers, and browsing in news sites on the Web. It thus seems inevitable that in time the Net will become the de facto corporate training resource, superior both in currency and cost-effectiveness to the various forms of management training and education now available (and on which an estimated $40 billion is spent annually). Executives will no longer have to give up time they can ill afford to lose attending three-day, off-site lecture programs to keep up with change.

Until very recently, the mass (broadcast) media established dominant brands of products: they are the underpinning for consumer marketing as we know it today. In the bustle of the dynamic, participatory marketplace that lies ahead of us, the nature of branding will be subject to profound change as companies adopt other ways of attracting and retaining consumers' attention and patronage.

The real time message:

The new digital media fundamentally change the old broadcast model for communication between institutions and society to one of access. In business, succeeding with these media calls for both imagination and vision—the former to discover and explore uncharted space, the latter to lead in new, real time ways of engaging consumers. Engagement is dialogue: the new digital media will deliver information wrapped in forms of interactive entertainment.

What's in a name?

—WILLIAM SHAKESPEARE, *Romeo and Juliet*, 1594–1595

We know a lot about how brands have
worked in the past. But now more than
ever, there is evidence that our knowledge
of brands isn't enough for these times.

—YOUNG & RUBICAM EXECUTIVE, *Advertising
Age International*, September 19, 1994

4 A Brand New Brand

IGITAL TOOLS have finally given
marketing the means to live up to
its top-dog billing. Management
gurus of all stripes have for more than two
decades been pronouncing that marketing,
the customer's advocate in corporations, no
longer merely defines the way an organization
attracts buyers but determines the way a
company does business. Yet by comparison with
production, engineering, product design, and
accounting, this managerial function has until now

been instinctive, vague, and suppositional in its methods—as if performed by some mysterious creative means, if not with smoke and mirrors. Marketing, the customer's advocate, has been able to supply little concrete evidence that it knows those customers very well and that it could, therefore, direct the rest of the organization to give customers what they want.

If marketing has addressed customers en masse, through broadcast media, that is because it could no more "see" them as individuals than a speaker high on a platform addressing a vast audience of blurry faces. The best it could do, in trying to present management with a sharper image, was to commission market research, studies that often take a month or two for approval, three months of preparation, two months of field work, and another two months of analysis. Forget real time. After that, marketing "gatekeepers"— as Dave Power of J. D. Power & Associates once described them to me— would debate whether or not to release the data. In consequence, most market research studies were no more than hit-or-miss exercises in justifying decisions already made, by the seat of the pants, on how to tackle a market.

Fortunately, that modus operandi is now seriously out of date. Technology—and in particular, the on-line technology of the Internet in all its various forms and offshoots—has made it possible for companies to be in touch with their customers individually and in real time. With systems like this, a company is often aware of what customers are doing as they do it, can virtually know what customers are thinking from moment to moment, and can give them immediate attention tailored to their particular needs. The gatekeepers of stale, marginally useful market research material are being put out of work by live marketing databases to which everyone in a company can get access—the chairman of the board and the marketing VP as well as a far-flung junior regional manager—at virtually the same instant a salesperson with a laptop out in the field logs on to enter data gathered from a customer seated beside her.

Brand Redefined for the Information Age

For both marketing theory and practice, the most dramatic implication of this shift to real time marketing is the complete transformation of the concept of brand. Once brand was simply about product differentiation. Successful brand names commanded unquestioned loyalty, and they were created chiefly by advertisements broadcast by mass media. These one-way messages were absorbed—often subliminally—by consumers who took them to be virtual instructions on what to buy and where to buy it. Brands had the effect of "reducing or eliminating the need to find out about a product before buying it," as one marketing primer put it.[1] But all that is now history. Branding of a new and entirely different kind is being born—brand as *an encapsulation of actual, experienced value*. The nature of that experience is increasingly determined through customer preferences expressed in dialogue with producers or service providers—an exchange made possible by technology, and one in which the consumer has the upper hand.

The turnabout has a curious parallel on the wider stage of society at large, a parallel that, in an illustration of art reflecting life, showed up in a trend in literary fiction. In 1970s and early 1980s America, the reigning school of contemporary literature was known as minimalism. At first this writing was much admired for being something like the literary equivalent of photorealism in painting—startlingly true to life in its smallest details: characters did not simply order sodas but Pepsis or Cokes; did not loll in recliners but in La-Z-Boys; did not roar away in pickups but in Ford or Chevy trucks. By the mid- to late 1980s, when the genre began to fall out of favor with literary critics, it came to be known as Kmart fiction (stories in which people did not walk into any old store but a Kmart, Sears, etc.). One principal objection to the genre was that it described a cultural landscape whose most prominent features appeared to be commercial brand names—a shallow society shaped by corporate America's image manipulators. It was fiction weak in drama and characterization and almost bereft of plot, the critics complained, depicting Americans as lacking faith in everything but the material dimension of life, or things defined by brand names.

Meanwhile, technology had begun to supply the means for a sort of reverse sculpture, in which society would define the goals and agendas of corporate America. Thanks to technological progress, media tools used to manipulate people's minds could be employed to bend corporate America to society's will.

People Aren't Going to Take It Any More

Society, at present, shows every sign of being sicker than ever before of old-fashioned, image-mongering brand marketing. In England, for instance, two researchers at the Manchester Business School (www.mbs.ac.uk) recently drew attention to the staggering difference between the cost structures of the most and least expensive makers of sunflower margarine. The total manufacturing costs, plus profit, of the upscale, branded product was more than six times higher than that of the unbranded, "private label," lowest priced brand. As quoted in the *Financial Times*, one of the researchers wondered if

> brand imagery [could] continue to sustain the differences in the prices shoppers pay for similar or even inferior products.... As shoppers become more sophisticated, more willing to trust the retailer to provide products of adequate quality irrespective of the name they carry, many manufacturers of grocery products are likely to have to reduce their internal costs.[2]

Commenting on the Manchester study in the *Financial Times* article, a senior executive at the U.K. Unilever subsidiary that sells Britain's best-selling brand of margarine correctly pointed out that this particular criticism of brand is an old one (www.tasteyoulove.com). What is different now is that the most progressive companies serving consumers are finally taking steps to reduce their dependence on brand marketing drastically. Instead, they are winning over consumers by ascertaining and responding to their real needs, not the least of these being their wish for fewer brands.

Leading this switch is the company with the most hallowed name in conventional brand marketing, Procter & Gamble (www.pg.com), which has long specialized in pushing several brand identities—a variety of selling pitches tailored to the susceptibilities of different market segments—for virtually the same product. As a front-page article in the *Wall Street Journal* reported early in 1997, P&G recognized that its 440 promotions a year for 110 brands—which often involved making fifty-five price changes a day—were only confusing customers.[3] Customers did not, for instance, want the thirty-five kinds of Bounce fabric softener sold in North America alone. This excess of variety amounted to foisting on consumers choices that P&G thought they *should* want—what I call broadcast marketing— rather than choices for which consumers had expressed an actual need. In this case what consumers did need was fewer promotions and less choice. As noted in the article, "Today's average consumer…has less time to browse; it is down 25 percent from five years ago." This consumer typically spends twenty-one minutes buying "an average of 18 items, out of 30,000 to 40,000 choices."[4]

This is not, as it might appear to be, a contradiction of my observation in chapter 2 that consumers expect to be given even more choice in the future than they have now. Consumers always want more choice, but consumers burdened by choice, as they often are today, begin to look for *meaningful* choice, or choice that better reflects what they really do want or need at any particular moment. Hence the same *Wall Street Journal* article notes that although one P&G customer, Giant Food, an East Coast chain of 174 supermarkets, is cutting down on baby-related products and detergents in response to its shoppers' preferences, customer preferences also led the chain to expand the variety of Pringles chips it carried from two to five.

Consumers always want more choice, but they don't want to be burdened by it.

P&G has redirected its effort from marketing brand names to building close relationships with retailers that enable them to benefit from grocery stores' knowledge of and insights into customer behavior. Most significantly,

*after 159 years, P&G is changing the name of its Sales Depart-
ment to Customer Business Development, a change that may
seem largely symbolic but that within a tradition-bound company such as Procter & Gamble is a watershed event. The company decided it is wiser to let consumers drive supply than to
force-feed retailers by making them buy more products than
they can sell.*[5]

We Still Love Our Factories
More Than We Love Our Customers

The practice of burying retailers and customers under moun-
tains of products and promotions that P&G has begun to
reverse has, of course, been standard in consumer marketing.
Technology—applied to production and market segmentation—is responsible for this interment, but technology—
applied to communication—will also take the credit for disin-
terring consumers.

The old-style brand was a brilliant device for encouraging
mass consumption of mass-produced things, a cornucopia of
low-cost, commodity-like goods among which brands served to
create largely illusory differences. That approach had its heyday
between 1980 and 1990, when production capacity in both
the United States and Japan grew more than 100 percent. This
turned almost all industries into "factory-driven" businesses
churning out products at the fastest rate in history. Industry
cheered the rise of new distribution channels, direct marketing,
catalog sales, giant malls, and superstores because these quickly
multiplying outlets for goods kept factories, with their hugely
expanded capacity, fully occupied.

But competition also intensified, and that put extraordinary
pressure on marketing. Companies looked to marketing to keep
the factories at full capacity by inventing new markets, creating

demand, and moving their products. Much of the burden actually fell on advertising, on which almost $180 billion is still spent each year in the United States. Advertising agencies, as the architects of brand image, came to be seen as the ultimate generators of demand and, in the increasingly turbulent competitive environment, were hired and fired more frequently.

Some surprisingly large companies have yet to get the message that this production-driven model for selling is counterproductive. After years of meager profit margins, the world's largest company, General Motors (www.gm.com), rolled out in 1996 an anachronistic marketing strategy intended to boost earnings. To this end, GM had hired specialists from Procter & Gamble with experience marketing detergent and mouthwash. Predictably, the new strategy turned on brand-based product differentiation, founded on advertising. This approach was intended to publicize not only the differences between GM vehicles and those of rivals but the differences between the autos and trucks of GM's own Buick, Oldsmobile, and Chevrolet divisions.

Arguably, if the company had over the years established intense two-way communication with customers, the differences between its models would be both attractive and obvious to prospective buyers (because those differences would reflect what those customers had said they wanted). GM would then hardly have needed to turn to the broadcast marketing method of advertising, which was of dubious value in any case because of automobile industry experts' concern about GM's sluggish rate of new product introduction and its relatively leisurely pace of production. Company management justified this slowness as necessary to improving the quality of its products. But the trade-off betrays GM's production-driven mentality, whose golden age was the 1950s and 1960s. A market-driven company, properly oriented for the millennium, would know it could not afford the luxury of focusing on quality at the expense of timeliness. This is simply not an option in the age of real time, in which *now* is probably the most critical aspect of *good* in consumers' minds.

Though the penalties of GMs' factory-focused management model have been noted for some time, and on many fronts, *Manufacturing Systems* reported in 1992 that GM had spent $40 billion on factory automation in the 1980s and yet still lagged in productivity.[6] In 1996, a study by the consulting firm of Harbour & Associates in Troy, Michigan, suggested the dimensions of the competitive disadvantage GM had created for itself through its insistence on making 70 percent of its own car components, compared with Ford's 50 percent and Chrysler's 30 percent. GM's labor costs for car components were $440 higher, per vehicle, than Ford's and $600 higher than Chrysler's.[7]

In addition, because of the company's obsession with manufacturing, marketing at GM, as at many auto companies, failed to move with the times. Dave Power told me that whereas computer-aided design and manufacturing have significantly cut costs in the industry, costs allocated to transportation, marketing, advertising, and incentives have remained high. They account for 30 percent of total costs and are still rising. Power added,

> *That is about $6,000 per car. That number has grown, yet the marketing people are frightened of changing the status quo. I was at a meeting in Europe recently where the head of one of the large auto manufacturers said, "It used to be that marketing chided manufacturing for being too conservative and backward. Now it is marketing that is unwilling to change and is seen as being in the Dark Ages."*[8]

Yet even high-technology companies that consider the automakers to be dinosaurs are themselves guilty of factory-driven rather than modern marketing. And they are justly

New Brand Is Information Rich

Interactive information technology will become the next major investment for the enterprise, giving consumers the power to choose and shape brand relationships with suppliers.

The illustration below is based on the idea that products and services are information dependent and that customer loyalty is enhanced by dialogue. At the low end of the scale, products such as Pepsi or Coke are interchangeable and disposable. There is little or no cost to the consumer for failing to make the right choice. At the top end, in the service sphere, is heart surgery—a complex, information-intensive, and high-risk "purchase decision."

With exceptionally high-risk, high-cost decisions, the consumer makes the greatest personal investment in service.

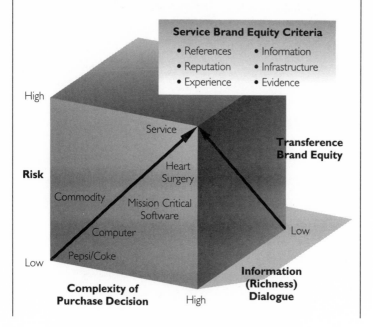

We choose a surgeon, a family pediatrician, a lawyer, a banker, or an investment broker with considerably more care than we buy soapsuds or even cars.

Heart surgery requires a good deal of work on the part of both the consumer and the service provider. It is a service with a standard base of know-how, but totally customized and personalized. Buyers of this service want a surgeon with a good reputation and usually find one by means of reference or referral. They want the additional insurance of having the surgery done at a reputable hospital, so the surgeon's entire support system—or the institutional "infrastructure"—is important. Information and dialogue are part of the purchase process. There is a great deal of interaction after the service has been rendered, and the consumer is reassured by the knowledge that he or she can always ask for and receive additional help or information. Because service is an intangible offering, tangible "evidence" must be given by the provider in order to reduce risk. Tangible evidence may take the form of personal references, customer lists, the "look and feel" of the product and service environment, or the knowledge of the salesperson.

The third dimension on the chart shows information "richness" and what I call "transference," or the transfer of responsibility for the details of the "purchase" from the consumer to the judgment of the selling party. In the case of heart surgery, the physician makes a recommendation, and his or her judgment is usually accepted. So "transference" has to do with trust. Information, in a variety of forms, builds the evidence allowing transference to take place.

How, then, can this kind of trust be developed by suppliers dealing with millions of customers? Brand relationship development is different for different categories of producers. Developing a brand relationship for a microprocessor or a computer is not the same as doing it for soap or perfume. With products that are more costly, complicated, and subtly differentiated, the customer has more at stake. For example, when shopping for a car, the customer will consider price, quality, maintenance costs, resale value, design, safety, subjective appeal—all the aspects that make people pore over *Consumer Reports* and car magazines. The fast answer is, *Build sustaining presence and relationships with the customer that extend well beyond the point of sale.*

I like to pose these two questions in my marketing workshops: "How many times have you asked or been asked, 'What personal computer should I buy?'" I usually receive a show of hands from 80 to 90 percent of the audience in response to both questions. Both the psychological and the financial risks of buying a particular brand of computer are reduced by references. Products such as cars, appliances, computers, telephone systems, corporate databases, and entertainment systems are more like purchasing heart surgery than buying a Coke.

In the age of information and choice, all businesses will become more service-like, even those producing commodities such as soap and soft drinks. Detergent makers, using databases, the Internet, and 800 numbers, can offer consumers advice on cleaning and stain problems. Soft drink suppliers might plan parties or offer nutrition and diet counsel. Driven by the need to maintain customer loyalty and grasping the great advantage of the new information and communication tools, every product company will, in some way, become a service company.

criticized for rank insensitivity to consumers' needs. As the historian and social commentator Theodore Roszak complains, their products are maddeningly hard to use:

> *Many people are desperately trying to master the information superhighway these days because they hope there is a magic machine that will soothe their high-tech fury by telling them all they need to know about this big, confusing world. But what they find along the superhighway is more technological dependency: computer protocols, networking complexities and constantly shifting interfaces that are even harder to master than their VCR controls.*
>
> *…[C]omputers…[confront] us with ever-increasing levels of complexity. One brings the machine home only to discover within a few months time that nothing works as advertised. The parts are incompatible; the error messages that flash across the screen are as inscrutable as pronouncements by the oracle of Delphi.…[C]omputers are authentically hard to use. They are not well designed; the programs get bigger and glitchier and more time-consuming to learn with every upgrade.*[9]

Roszak's complaints are of course widespread. And consumers grow all the more baffled and enraged when high-tech companies make claims of "user friendly" or "easy-to-install" products.

Business Carves Up
Ever Smaller Pieces of the Pie

The first phase of the information age has actually exacerbated the factory-driven approach to marketing, even if it has brought sweeping changes to the way factories spew out their products and marketers go about finding homes for them. Computers, assisting with everything from design to distribution, have made it easier and cheaper to develop new products—and at wildly accelerated speeds (three months, for instance, for products that used to take three years from conception to manufacture). Computers have also made it possible to turn out goods in smaller, higher-quality lots and to distribute them more efficiently. And they have allowed producers to cater profitably to ever-narrower market segments. Databases slice markets into every imaginable grouping; flexible design and production methods are used to supply what companies think, often inaccurately, that this segment or that one wants. Procter & Gamble, for example, only recently discovered that mothers did not want his and hers diapers, which it promptly replaced with unisex Pampers.

Because all companies have access to the same computer-based tools, competition has forced even laggards to adopt product and market segmentation. To compete with the latest segment-specific brands on the block, long-established companies have launched hosts of brand extensions—Old El Paso salsa from Pillsbury to fight El Paso Chile, a high-end gourmet salsa, and Red Dog ale from Miller Brewing Company to battle the products of the microbreweries. The curious result of the proliferation of computer-based tools capable of creating unprecedented diversity is that look-a-like products—from potato chips to computer chips—crowd ever-smaller market segments. The fragmentation of markets has been given extra impetus by the growing ranks of small companies supplying generic products and clones: because information technology has made it possible to cater to ever-tinier segments, these enterprises have been flourishing in small niches.

In a number of *Harvard Business Review* articles,[10] I have shown how these trends have combined in the 1990s to put obscure suppliers (often lumped together under the label "Other" in market share pie charts) in the position of significant and fast-growing competitors. It was once conventional wisdom to assume that over time industries inevitably consolidated, generics faded, and diversification subsided. But in fact, as dominant as Microsoft is in the PC software market, the largest market share for this product worldwide is still claimed by "Other."

These growing ranks of small operators, as well as large companies creating brand extensions, are deploying database segmentation and direct marketing techniques so precise as to be capable of addressing and targeting the smallest conceivable market—the market of one. Customers in their microsegments are being bombarded with promotional messages, delivered not just through familiar media such as print and network television advertisements, point-of-sale displays, talking table tents, catalogs, and phone calls but also fax broadcasts, on-line flashing messages, customized newsletters, e-mail, and in-flight commercials. Many customers are increasingly irritated by this onslaught; more and more they switch brands with impunity, overnight.

Brand New Marketing:
Child of the Information Age

How, in this environment, can companies create and maintain brand loyalty? The answer is to alter brand definition so as to supply what has been missing from the picture: a rich dialogue between producers and consumers, part of the feedback loop described in chapters 2 and 3. That producer-customer interaction, made possible by the tools of the information age, will need to have its information systems tuned to real time if companies are to coordinate and deliver finely calibrated, timely responses to consumers.

As I show in the next chapter, "The Real Time Corporation," this kind of response will require a new, keen attentiveness to customers as well as to customer-oriented investment in every sphere of corporate activity, from design to after-purchase service. Achieving closure on satisfying customer wants will be a struggle for marketing executives trying to inculcate in their organizations this real time approach to building brand strength. Time-honored biases will die hard. A Levi Strauss manufacturing manager I once heard being interviewed defined heaven as "One size fits all," only to be promptly corrected by his marketing counterpart, who offered as his own, rather different definition, "Every size and color made for the individual."

Some of today's best-managed corporations are already reaping the benefits of brand dominance forged, as it will be in the future, from exemplary customer consideration, even though their success is often attributed, quite wrongly, to old-fashioned image creation. Consider Intel, for instance (www.Intel.com). In many of the articles I have read about the "Intel Inside" brand-

Consumer-Producer Dialogue

Peter Drucker said that the "purpose of business is to satisfy customers." The new technologies allow for direct interaction between consumers and producers, disintermediating many of the people and functions in-between.

ing campaign, the success of Intel's brand is credited to the slogan and the size of the advertising budget. These articles fail to point out that Intel owned more than 80 percent of the microprocessor market before it began that campaign. It is not advertising but leadership won over the course of twenty years of technology development, carefully integrating customers' needs, that made Intel a household name.

The microprocessor "development systems" that Intel pioneered in the early 1970s helped engineers at customer companies design this customizable component into their new products more quickly and less painfully than was possible before its introduction. Taking a systems approach to product design, Intel added peripheral products and services, making the customer's job easier, allowing them to get their products to market faster. Competitors challenging Intel have long had to contend with the service-like marketing operation the company has developed, a rarity in the commodity-oriented semiconductor industry of which Intel is part. Intel's all but impregnable "infrastructure"—the assemblers, software developers, value-added resellers, and systems integrators, all of which had adopted Intel's architecture as the standard to which they fit their own products—has even made it hard for competitors with superior microprocessors to make a dent in Intel's dominant share of the market. Intel's huge investment in R&D and in production facilities also contributed to its brand strength: it out-innovated and out-invested its rivals.

Brand is more than a name. It represents a relationship customers have come to know and value.

In the same way, the slogans we all seem to have known forever—"Coke adds life" and "It's the Real Thing"—have had far less to do with the power of the Coca-Cola brand than the company's biggest brand asset—its peerless worldwide distribution (www.cocacola.com). P&G, held up as the ultimate authority on branding, is actually the beneficiary of generous spending on R&D and outstanding distribution that is heavily dependent on information technology to make sure that its products are always sitting on grocery store shelves right where and when customers want them.

Building a supportive infrastructure takes time, and without it, brand is meaningless. America Online (www.aol.com) found that out in early 1997, when what many pundits saw as a marvelous marketing effort turned sour. AOL offered access to its on-line services at one low standard rate, compelling net surfers to sign up by the tens of thousands, only to find a busy signal when they tried to log on. Angry consumers filed lawsuits, government agencies forced the company to give rebates and cut advertising, and a number of users switched to other providers. The promotion worked as intended, but the company's brand suffered.

New Brand High Touch

Brand is so much more than a static name in an ad or on a package linked to vague associations with promises, success, or the good life. Rather, brand is an active experience—a difference I was able to explain to my wife by contrasting experiences we each had on a single day.

The nature of my wife's work has made her heavily dependent on her cellular phone company, so a notification that she was about to have her service canceled came as a nasty shock that morning. It seems that her payment for her bill, which happens to be five times the national average, had not been received by the company. She had, in fact, paid what she owed by electronic funds transfer. To establish this, she was forced first to spend half an hour on hold waiting for a cellular company representative and then to have our bank fax confirmation of the payment to the billing department. The cellular service was unwilling to give her the benefit of the doubt, even though a supervisor subsequently confessed that it was because the company had changed its billing codes without informing its customers that her transfer of funds had gotten stuck in electronic limbo.

In the information age, all businesses will become service businesses.

Coincidentally I, too, had a late notice that day from American Express for a payment made electronically. I was heading out to Tokyo the next day and was concerned about not being able to use my card once I got there. As I explained all this to an American Express representative, I could hear the clicking of computer keys in the background as he looked up the history of my account. He asked where I was employed. "The McKenna Group," I replied, and noted that, as a very mobile consulting firm and an American Express client, we are a good customer. I vividly recall his response: "I can see that," he said. Because both my personal record and that of my firm were good, he said he would note that the payment was under dispute and should be given time to clear. "You can continue to use your card without any problems," he added (www.american express.com).

As I told my wife, the information technology behind American Express's instantaneous troubleshooting will be the key to determining the brand marketing winners and losers of the decade ahead: exceptional service is already linked inextricably to highly responsive, computer-based systems. I do not find it surprising that the chief information officers at two leaders in the use of computers for customer satisfaction, P&G and Federal Express, were promoted to their positions from marketing. Marketing management will have to become increasingly concerned with the minutiae of developing interactive information services. In fact, I believe that budgets for broadcast marketing will soon be reallocated to the information tools of interactive marketing: on-line connections, Web TV, computer kiosks, self-service terminals, and customer call centers.

A climate of innovation is transforming marketing from the ground up. Innovation, Peter Drucker says, "is an economic and social term. Its criterion is not science or technology, but a change in the economic or social environment—a change in the behavior of people as consumers or producers."[11] Businesses are

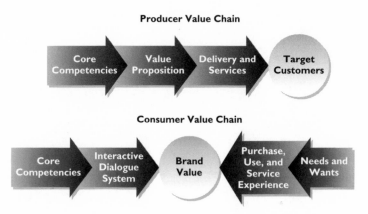

Producer versus Consumer Value

Traditional value chains look from the inside out, viewing the customer as a "target." Dialogue technologies create self-service, transparent interfaces, feedback, and twenty-four-hour interaction. The result is an information exchange through which both consumer and producer grow and learn in the process.

likely to discover that their customers are innovating or adapting faster than they are. Ultimately, the way to build brand muscle will be for marketing to catch up with customers' reorientation—and then, as my next chapter shows, for the rest of the organization to keep up with marketing.

The real time message:

Brand is a virtual experience derived from the consumer's experiences with the product, service, or company—not from the messages of broadcast media. The development of brand requires that an infrastructure of distribution, support, and service be in place when and where the consumer wants it. Real time technology delivers the brand experience anytime, anyplace.

The scrapping of rigid, moribund corporate hierarchies is vital to managing technology. Basically, that means making people talk to each other.

—*The Economist*, December 1989

Only connect!

—E. M. FORSTER, *Howard's End*, 1910

5 The Real Time Corporation

REAL TIME MANAGEMENT will mean transforming relationships inside companies. It calls for the intimate and immediate interconnection of marketing, product development, engineering, and manufacturing—in fact, of every sphere of an organization's activity.

The road to real time management is strewn with cautionary as well as inspirational tales, and I will begin with one of the former. It relates to an experience had by Apple Computer in the mid-

1990s, a time when the company was poised for a resurgence in the Intel-Microsoft–dominated personal computer marketplace.

A well-known American university ordered a few thousand Powerbook computers from Apple and announced that it would give these, free of charge, to newly enrolled students. Apple held a major share of the higher-education computer market, and the group tackling that market well understood its requirements. This group's annual forecast for the education market was combined with forecasts for all other segments of Apple's business, including sales to business and direct and retail sales. At Apple, as at other companies, the forecasts for a given year were constantly adjusted upward and downward according to various individual estimates, bonus incentives, and sales goals set by managers. Marketing and sales then estimated the total number of Powerbooks they believed could be bought in that year by adjusting the final sales forecast against historical sales goals and results.

After that, the factory had to have its say, and it hardly ever believed the forecasts from the field. Its own forecast was based not just on historical production and sales numbers but also on estimates of what it could handle—largely a function of component suppliers' lead times for delivery. As at many companies, the reconciliation of marketing and manufacturing numbers was a fractious process of guesses, estimates, alterations, debates, and compromises.

In this event, Apple found itself a million units short of demand that year, with most of the shortfall consisting of Powerbooks. The university that had used the offer of a free machine as a sign-up tactic had delighted prospective students and their parents, and their reaction helped the institution to attain its enrollment goal. But now this customer had to be told that it would get only a tenth of the computers it wanted. Word came back down the chain to the Apple salesman on the spot, and then to the university officials, only a few weeks before the start of the fall semester. The head of the university called the president of Apple demanding that he do something. Powerbooks were duly reallocated to the university, but some people somewhere else had to be severely disappointed. With Apple unable either to gauge demand accurately or to adjust marketing's optimism to manufacturing's production constraints, customer satisfaction and confidence suffered.

All the brand recognition and sexy product design in the world were of little use to Apple without a reliable demand-supply balancing information system. Anyone looking for real customer demand numbers or real production capacity had nowhere in the company to go. The irony here is that Apple, as an information company, had the knowledge and the technologies for deploying an information system relating manufacturing estimates to marketing data, in real time. Of course, Apple's experience is hardly unique. Many high- and low-tech companies continue to base their demand-supply forecasts on individual judgments, without the benefit of any factual information about what has been actually ordered and what factory capacity is any particular time.

Orchestrating Connectivity

Marketing, in its pivotal, turn-of-the-century role as the representative and advocate of customers, has at its disposal tools of unprecedented power in their capacity to orchestrate a company's responsiveness to those customers. These tools go well beyond what has traditionally been thought of as marketing's purview. They have the power to create customer loyalty and satisfaction exceeding anything possible with the strictly promotional tools of the past. They underpin the workings of the adaptive or real time corporation and have to be accessible throughout the extended enterprise. Their outstanding feature is connectivity.

The most impressive accomplishments of computerization in business to date have been concentrated in creating a manufacturing environment characterized by shorter design cycles and flexible retooling. Marketing and sales, by contrast, have been virtually untouched by technological progress and have carried on much as they have for decades. Though computers have been used to crunch sales data and to generate five- and ten-year market forecasts, conventional forecasting has become increasingly pointless in an environment of accelerated, multi-directional, unending metamorphosis—in which Netscape, for instance, has been introducing new versions of its Web browser software every four months in its war with the powerful Microsoft, which has been developing products at an equally fast clip (up to the late 1990s, software of comparable complexity was updated only every year or two).

In companies honing their competitive edge for the twenty-first century, marketing has to meet the following real time requirements.

Analyze customer feedback constantly—with that feedback originating in many instances from customers closely tied to a company's operations.

The high-tech pioneers of integration of this degree were Sil-icon Valley suppliers of subassemblies and their customers—makers of computer systems and silicon foundries turning out custom chips. Berkeley scholar AnnaLee Saxenian noted in 1990 that some computer systems firms in the valley "even include[d] suppliers in their design review meetings."[1]

Act on that customer feedback, which calls for dynamic collabo-ration—based on shared information—between all of a company's departments and managerial functions, as well as its suppliers and customers.

As Saxenian notes, in the case of Silicon Valley computer systems manufacturers and their suppliers, such cooperation "allows the supplier to adapt its products to anticipated market changes and exposes the systems engineers to changing com-ponent technologies."[2]

Closely monitor the quality and speed of a company's responsive-ness to customer feedback.

The computer technology making all of this possible is only now beginning to be widely disseminated. Today, earlier gener-ations of information processing systems and structures are actually getting in the way of real time management.

For example, a frequent observation by my friend Ali Kutay—president of Formtek, an enterprise software services subsidiary of Lockheed whose clients have included Nike and Volvo—is that surprisingly large and well-known companies are still run by a mainframe-centered managerial infrastructure. An excess of centralized control and cumbersome, user unfriendly soft-ware interfaces discourage executives from gleaning more than a fraction of the information that resides in corporate databases.

Such systems are as far from real time tools as they could possibly be. On the other hand, the client-server–based systems that have been replacing or supplementing mainframes in many corporations also present obstacles to bringing management fully up to date. If the mainframe's principal drawback was excessive centralization, the chief disadvantage of client-server networks—in which computing tasks are distributed among smaller, linked machines with a "server" acting as the repository of files and programs shared by a number of "client" computers—is excessive fragmentation. Instead of one great big and inhibiting company database, client-server systems often spawn numerous unrelated databases that make it difficult for different departments of companies to collaborate or for data to be shared across databases.

Networked Computers:
The Connective Tissue between
People and Information

Prototypes of real time information systems of the future—which have the drawbacks of neither mainframes nor client-server networks—are springing up in much the same guerrilla fashion as personal computers did in large corporations in the early 1980s. For an interface, these systems borrow the World Wide Web browser format or, specifically, a collection of easy-to-use software conventions—from the so-called hypertext markup language (HTML)—that allow managers to link and share information simply by clicking on words, phrases, and even photographs, videos, and animations. Effectively in-house equivalents of the Internet, these systems are known as intranets.

Easy access to pick, click, and share applications by any team or manager collaborating across an intranet came in 1995, with Sun Microsystems' introduction of the Java programming language. Java is an object-oriented language that frees users from having to concern themselves with the arcana of computer programming—such as incompatible operating systems or

The Intranet, Extranet, and Internet

Real time corporate communications consist of three spheres: the intranet, linking the vital resources within the company and protected by an information firewall; the extranet, linking an enterprise's extended family of suppliers, distributors, retailers, and partners; and the Internet, an open, free-ranging array of millions of computer hosts providing information on competitors, government activity, the media, and academia. Corporations, in the future, will use their networks to develop the infrastructure and communities of interest necessary for sustaining customer loyalty and brand equity.

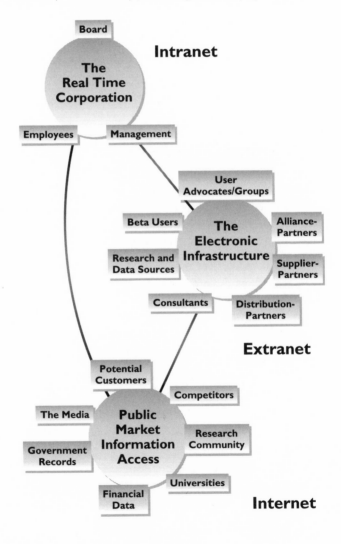

hardware of different machines on the network—making networking technology "transparent" to them. Java works as if all the software commands and translations a user needs to access specific pieces or types of information are automatically included and executed in the act of requesting them. Overall, it means that through computers all employees can at any time get an overview of the entire company; that computers can show each employee how his or her contribution affects the organization from day to day or month to month; that hot new ideas and information can be shared with colleagues immediately.

In real time corporations, data stored on intranets will not sit around waiting to be distributed to different sections of the company but will be made freely and dynamically available to all managers. The inventor of HTML, Doug Engelbart, who back in the 1960s conceived of networked computers as the connective tissue between people and information, envisages "collaborative hypertext documents" in which project reports, e-mail, and video footage, including teleconferencing snippets, are linked and easily accessible.

As Ali Kutay puts it,

> What's the relationship between a project schedule and the manufacturing or marketing information you need to complete it? Dynamism! That's the interesting thing about this whole generation of computing. It's about content being constantly referred to other content. Discrete elements of information— buying schedules, design documents, specifications, order forms, budgets—have to be linked to other discrete information elements to become useful.[3]

One of Ali's customers—a $4 billion corporation we will call Company Q—has begun to use a rudimentary version of this sort of information system, which joins the information resources of two historically antagonistic internal organizations, manufacturing and engineering. Before the new system was set up, the two even maintained separate and inconsistent bills of materials. This procedural divergence considerably complicated manufacturing's job of rendering the designs of the engineers "manufacturable"—and of making sure that new products fit the company's quality standards, procurement procedures, and budgets. Senior managers would not touch this highly charged control issue for fear of curtailing the engineers' autonomy.

With a newly installed Web-based intranet, however, manufacturing and engineering began to look at each other's procedures and specifications and to exchange information routinely, in real time. They took steps toward agreeing on a common bill of materials system. Though the old tensions have not vanished entirely, engineers are now able to plug into their designs the components that manufacturing actually uses to implement production, and manufacturing managers are able to check and see if they can make the new designs efficiently. By taking advantage of information-sharing tools of real utility, the company has altered human behavior—almost subliminally—in a way that could not have been done if it had simply ordered the battling departments to cooperate across the boundaries of their traditional compartments and antipathies.

Real time communication can break down barriers between traditional adversaries within the company.

Indeed, once people get used to working in this collaborative fashion, the technology that has catapulted them into the age of real time will become just as invisible as other technological agents have throughout history. The now-ubiquitous fractional horsepower motors—in our vacuum cleaners, refrigerators, electric shavers, blenders, and hair dryers—for which we scarcely ever spare a thought, were not hidden inside appliances sixty years ago. They were independent devices requiring special installation and skilled deployment, with the aid of specialized attachments.

When intranets become as unobtrusive as miniature motors, managers with different specializations not only will be sharing information but will effectively be working *inside* the same store of data. These managers might be separated by oceans and continents, and the data will be adapted to keep up with shifting events and changing inputs from second to second, if need be. In effect, the boundaries of time and space that today limit the scope of work will disappear.

The Effects of Real Time on Employee Interaction

The changes in the way people in corporations work as a consequence of real time technologies will be taken for granted and as little remarked on as the transformative technologies that are responsible for them. What form will these changes take? There are some hints in the findings of two researchers who have devoted years to studying how computer networks change patterns of communication in organizations. They have found, for instance, that networks encourage people to talk more frankly and that networked groups generate more proposals for action than do teams conferring in more conventional ways. In fact, networks tend to have a democratizing effect, which suggests how real time organizations are likely to evolve.

For their study, the researchers observed groups of both high- and low-ranking employees make decisions by electronic mail and face to face. They concluded that the opinions of higher-status people carried less clout and were paid less attention when the medium of communication was electronic mail:

> Networked communication is only beginning to affect the structure of the workplace.... [Today] formal command structures specify who reports to whom, who assigns to whom and who has access to what information.... Organizations are traditionally built around two key concepts: hierarchical decomposition of goals and tasks and the stability of employee relationships over time. In the fully networked organization that may become increasingly common in the future, task structures may be much more flexible and dynamic. Hierarchy will not vanish, but it will be augmented by distributed lattices of interconnections.[4]

The researchers found other effects they had not anticipated. For example:

> The discretionary information sharing at...networked organizations seems to run contrary to nonelectronic behavior in organizations. [Employees] openly admit their ignorance to perhaps hundreds or even thousands of people. The repliers respond to requests for help from people they do not know with no expectations of any direct benefit to themselves....Respondents seem to believe that sharing information enhances the overall electronic community and leads to a richer information environment. The result is a kind of electronic altruism quite different from the fears that networks would weaken the social fabric of organizations.[5]

Yet even if e-mail does bring about deep and subtle changes in organizational life, it will soon seem the most prosaic medium for corporate communication. New forms of TV-like "socializing media" will bind employees together inside companies even more powerfully, just as they will enrich exchanges between companies and customers. Businesses will be able to apply techniques from entertainment and deploy systems resembling TV programming—over intranets and the Internet, or over outside extensions of corporate communications called extranets—to educate and train employees, announce new products, hold interactive customer seminars and workshops, and collaborate with other companies. They will effectively end up with thousands of new media "channels" for narrowcasting to small, specific audiences—some within, some outside, their corporate bounds.

When Is a Task Done?

For marketing taking its cues from customers' wants and reactions, the real time tool with the most radical benefits has to do with measurement. Virtually every company in business for a few years has had the experience of introducing a new product or service that failed—and of discovering, in analyzing its lack of success, that it did not incorporate features that market intelligence and marketing managers had, at the start, described as essential to market acceptance. Somewhere between marketing's listing of requirements and the product or service launch, the details were lost or ignored or compromises unacceptable to marketing managers were made without their knowledge. There was, in fact, no checklist or measure of "doneness"—the degree to which marketing's specifications were acted on. In fact, when people in companies say they are "done," they have often met only two-thirds or less of their own criteria for completing a job—whether the work concerned has to do with engineering, financial, or marketing management.

> When people say they are "done" with a job, they have rarely met all the necessary requirements.

The real time solution to this problem is to begin by setting up a project database into which is fed all the linked deadlines and other performance goals of every member of the team assembled for the exercise. At any stage, any manager from any department can access the schedule of progress—at higher or lower levels of detail—and get real time information about where things stand. An executive can see when some procedure or system is not working and take corrective action—which may even include training employees in skills they have been found to lack. Even more important in certain businesses is the option of allowing customers to make similar verifications for themselves (for example, checking the status of an order by logging onto a company's order management computer network). Federal Express put such a system in place in November 1994, allowing customers on the World Wide Web to track their own shipments on the FedEx package-tracking database.

As Ali Kutay sees it,

> One of the interesting things about this automation is that it forces people to go back and think about their business processes. What's the definition of "done"? Have you done the quality checks? Have you done enough testing? And so on. What companies discover as they go about this exercise is that the same employees who define what "done" is themselves fail to execute the necessary steps involved—but the system draws attention to their oversights. All of a sudden companies are getting real time information about what is actually happening in their organizations—they don't get nasty surprises six months later when, maybe, customers call and say, "What is this? Take it back! Fix it!" Or whatever.[6]

This sort of capability will be indispensable to the company that wants to keep track of its constant adaptations to customer wants and demands—to monitor the unending process of communication, action, and evaluation that goes on within the closed-loop system that is the real time corporation. Information moves from the market to customer service and marketing to product development and manufacturing and then back out again to the company's family of customers and suppliers.

Feedback and Self-Service Are the Touchstones of the Real Time Corporation

Although no single company has yet completed the transition to real time management, several have negotiated important early stepping stones.

- **Intuit:** Realizing that the ultimate goal of real time management is to give customers the means to satisfy themselves, Intuit (www.Intuit.com), the personal finance software specialist, introduced a product-service hybrid designed to speed customer satisfaction. Quicken Live, related to Intuit's best-selling personal finance software package, Quicken, contains additional software—an on-line connection and a browser. At the click of a button, users get onto the Quicken network and are instantly able to customize the program to their wants or needs. Because the 10 million Quicken users can serve themselves, they derive satisfaction in real time, sharply reducing Intuit's customer-support costs (see the interview with Bill Campbell of Intuit). Ideas for changes in applications come from a well-established feedback loop.

- **Wal-Mart:** At Wal-Mart (www.wal-mart.com), which has divided the United States into seventeen sales regions but

Bill Campbell of Intuit (www.Intuit.com)

In 1996, Intuit, the pioneer in personal finance packages for per-sonal computer users, had an estimated 10 million customers for its top-selling program, Quicken. Intuit's annual sales had grown from $210 million in 1994—when Bill Campbell became CEO—to $539 million in 1996, an expansion rate owed partly to a hand-ful of small acquisitions. Bill Campbell explained Intuit's modus operandi to me.

Our products are relatively bug-free—after all, it's not like these are rocket science products with millions of bytes of code. But the challenge we face is designing these things so people can use them as effortlessly as possible. As good as we are at product design, when people begin to interact with our software many of them call up and say, "I'm confused—help!" So we have to address usability issues. Every year, we put out products and then start to get feedback for next year's ver-sions of them. What we want is to be able to satisfy users more immediately with ideas for adaptations and modifica-tions you can get neither from market research nor from usability tests prior to the launch of a product. So we're devel-oping Quicken Live, which will give us the ability to, for instance, update the help files, so that people having problems reading the manual can go on-line and download them, or download patches or fixes for products.

With real time comes the ability for a lot of self-help. A customer who needs support can get onto our Web site and say, "I can read that pretty much for myself, it's straightforward, and click on a button and it's right there for me! Why should I make that phone call?" And Intuit wins. We are of course spending less of our money on technical support, which can range from 10 to 15 percent of a product's revenue. We are able to spend more on R&D. We can spend more on hiring new people, and so on.

Now the next step is Quicken through subscription. That's being able to provide customers with whole updates and new features on a modular basis—downloading modules from us on-line. You can have a tax-planning module, an investment module. You want one that's going to help you track insurance? That, too. So all of those things are what we are really working our butts off for—mostly to satisfy our 10 million customers who want to use the product more and more fully.

has no regional sales offices, regional managers travel through their territory every week, meeting store managers, observing shoppers, and visiting competitor stores. Every Thursday they gather around a table at corporate headquarters in Bentonville, Arkansas, to discuss what they have seen and heard and to go over the analyses of sales data gathered from checkout scanners all over the country every day. On Fridays they go on the company's private television network with all the store managers to plan the following week.

• *Microsoft:* At Microsoft (www.microsoft.com), where, according to Bill Gates, 80 percent of product improvements are based on customer feedback, software developers listen in on calls from buyers of the products they have designed to gather unfiltered reactions from the marketplace. There is a built-in penalty for listening in but failing to respond appropriately. "To get the attention of our product group managers," Gates has explained, "we charge their departments for the cost of providing technical support to customers who use their products."[7]

- *Boston Chicken:* Two prototypes being tested at Boston Market, the chain of fast-food stores owned by Boston Chicken, are a real time employee feedback system and a customer feedback channel found on in-store kiosks. At the end of each shift, employees punching out on time clocks are encouraged to tap into computers to answer questions designed to ensure that they find their work "fun and rewarding." Their replies remain confidential, and store managers see a weekly analysis of the strengths and weaknesses of their branches. In the customer kiosk system, a touchscreen computer terminal sits beside store exits. Boston Chicken hopes customers on their way out the door will complete a thirty-second survey of their opinions on the food, service, hygiene, and so on.

  The premise behind both systems is that the freshest information is the most valuable. The company's early appreciation of the importance of real time feedback, and the systems to support it, could explain why its founding president, J. Bruce Harreld, was appointed senior vice-president of strategy at IBM in 1995.

- *Federal Express:* Federal Express (www.fedex.com) has been teaching its customers the skills they need to serve themselves. The company estimates that each year it trains an average of half a million users of its self-service Power Ship system, installed either on PCs it supplies to corporate customers for their use or on machines of their own. Most of these are not end customers but companies using FedEx to serve customers of their own. As noted above, in one of the most recent stages of the company's progression to real time operation, FedEx has been allowing everyone, including end customers, to log onto its database through the World Wide Web (see the interview with Dennis Jones of FedEx).

Dennis Jones of FedEx (www.fedex.com)

Dennis Jones, chief information officer at Federal Express, began his career as a CPA. After he joined the courier service, he worked in business planning and sales, then took over the direction of the company's information systems management. In an extraordinary testimonial to FedEx's dependence on computers, Dennis has integrated 250 of his information technologists into the company's sales force. He told me why.

We have almost 100,000 of our PCs placed with customers. We also have over 350,000 customers on the software version of [the self-service program] Power Ship placed on their PCs, turning those machines into Power Ships when they need to be. So, between hardware and software installs, we have a proprietary point-of-sale terminal base of over 450,000 PCs.

What we've attempted to do is, in effect, allow people to provide customer service to themselves. It's not a matter of off-loading the work but of letting them choose the kind of service they want to provide for themselves. Probably what is the hit in all this is that our customers, generally, are not the end customer. They are serving someone else. What we intended to do is to give our customers a very rich set of capabilities to serve their customers even better.

My guess is that we have probably trained more people to use an on-line environment than any other company in the world in the last ten years. We train an average of six users per Power Ship every year. And if we have 100,000 installs just on the hardware side, that's half a million people a year that we train to be on-line. We do this, in part, by placing some 250 IT people who work directly for me in the field with our sales team.

What we have found is that people love it, and they are constantly bringing to us ways in which we can improve the capabilities we brought to them. We've been doing this for almost ten years now. We probably have a bigger backlog of enhancements that users want than we did five or ten years ago.

What we attempt to do is, one, listen very closely to our sales force and IT support people as they train our customers and integrate our systems with theirs. We listen to the feedback they get when they are doing the training and after they make the installs. Two, we take thousands of calls a day from a help-desk standpoint, from people calling to ask about certain procedures. Or they may be new and may need additional training and so forth. The help desk serves not just as a means to solve problems but as a feedback channel. Three, we do formal customer satisfaction studies every quarter, and the report we get back looks like a Manhattan phone book. We seek feedback on enhancements we make. We get it from contacts made through our formal customer satisfaction surveys, we get it from telephone contacts, and we get it through face-to-face contact, when our sales and support people are on-site.

For our own internal management, the e-mail capabilities of the company are the most mission-critical system that we have—even before our package tracking and billing systems. About 90,000 of our total of 120,000 employees spread out across approximately 210 countries are on our e-mail system. I can't tell you the number of phone calls I have been able to kill off over this last year by using the Web and e-mail.

• **Kennametal:** One of my favorite comeback stories concerns a steel company in a small town fifty miles east of Pittsburgh that extended information technology to its customers to resurrect the business. Kennametal (www.kennametal.com) is the dominant industry in Latrobe, home of golfing great Arnold Palmer and where I happened to attend college for a few years. The company manufactures tools and products for the metalworking, mining, and highway construction industries.

Like many of the basic steel companies in America, Kennametal fell on tough competitive times in the twenty years leading up to the 1980s. At that time they began investing seriously in information technology and consequently emerged in the 1990s as one of America's most successful high-tech low-tech companies. A *New York Times* article in 1992 reported, "Kennametal's information systems have more in common with trend-setters in retailing, banking and transportation than those of most of its peers. They spent three years developing an information system so managers and customers could find out in seconds what products are available to them at their sites around the country." Little wonder, the company's very profitable revenues grew from $618 million in 1992 to more than $1 billion in 1996.[8]

It's Possible to Reach Critical Mass without Mass Confusion

There is no question that the many and vast transformations that real time technologies ask of organizations are paralyzing the managers of many companies, who seem much like deer caught in blazing headlights. It is not always easy to apply the embryonic technologies of real time. Computers have been in factories for decades, yet the ideal of the virtual factory—tens or hundreds of networked production facilities dividing labor so that each one does only what it does best, effectively working together as a single, well-oiled machine—remains hard to realize. As David Upton and Andrew McAfee point out in their essay "The Real Virtual Factory":

> [I]t is one thing for a networked factory to be possible or desirable, and it is quite another to create and maintain it and help it evolve. Designing the system, administering it, updating its technology, maintaining security, and exploiting new opportunities as they arise are collectively a huge job—and one that companies whose primary business is not IT will be loath to undertake.[9]

Yet once companies summon the will to tackle the job, their appetite for the new capabilities fast becomes ravenous—not to mention hugely contagious. Upton and McAfee offer the example of McDonnell Douglas Aerospace (www.mdc.com), which, with the help of a spin-off "information broker," AeroTech, built its virtual factory:

> [T]he number of participants in this computer-linked manufacturing community has soared since mid-1993, when AeroTech...began adding external suppliers to the network. Until then, the network had been limited to 50 or so McDonnell employees who used it to pass data between different computer systems within the organization. When external suppliers joined, they were so impressed with the way the network helped them work with McDonnell that they started to ask their suppliers and partners to join. By the fall of 1994, there were 400 internal and external users. There are now several thousand.[10]

This sort of sudden rash of implementation is very much of the hour—even if it is preceded by years of extreme technological conservatism (see the interview with Carmine J. Villani of McKesson).

In other cases, senior managers who resist change for too long are likely to be rocketed into the next evolutionary stage by

Carmine Villani, McKesson Corp.
(www.McKesson.com)

Carmine Villani is vice president of the Information Technology Division of McKesson Corp., a $14 billion, 164-year-old wholesale distributor of health care products and pharmaceuticals. In 1992, when Carmine Villani joined McKesson as vice president, he had put in twenty-seven years with IBM. His last title there was director of investment management. The job given to him by his new employer was to evaluate McKesson's IT and design a strategy for improving it.

In 1992, 70 percent of our systems were ten years old, or older, and 80 percent of the software applications were batch-processed. Even the on-line stuff was batch runs that were then just transmitted. I looked at the system's interfaces and found that 50 percent of the interfaces were literally paper—print out of one and whack it into another. We didn't have a single client-server application. This is just four short years ago.

Interestingly enough, McKesson had been an innovator in systems. In fact, back in 1980 or '82, it came out with the first hand-held order device in pharmacies and that definitely allowed it to leap ahead of the competition at the time. The bad news was that when competitors caught up five or six years later, they based their customer-ordering systems on the latest technology, whereas McKesson continued with a bunch of old technology.

When I arrived, the biggest problem was a lack of the right skills—we didn't have one person in the entire organization who had spent any time developing even the smallest client-server applications. I had to bring in a number of people from IBM, some at senior levels. The first project we worked on was the information warehouse—a huge inventory database with

112,000 different stock-keeping units (SKUs) serving 26,000 customers, so the combination of SKUs and customers was phenomenal. We put up an information warehouse on the mainframe, kind of dummied up, and we put a front end on it and made it available to the business. As soon as we did that, within two months, it was out of capacity because everyone who touched it wanted to use it and wanted more of it.

It's one thing to try and push an application or a technology on a business and another thing entirely to have the business pull it from you, the latter being the desirable thing.

So we brought this system in and got it up and running over a period of about three months, and that was about a year and a half ago. Since then, we have tied up our major customers to the warehouse. Rather than send them reports, we have given them direct links to their data inside the warehouse: they have their sales history with major chains; they have every store broken down, every department.

Next, we automated our sales force. We rolled out the sales automation project in which we gave Thinkpads to every one of our salespeople, with a whole suite of tools to enable them to manage their piece of the business, different wrinkles for the retail sales force versus the hospital sales force. We constantly update what they have on the toolkit, and they are constantly feeding us information on what they would like us to be able to do. We roll out new applications in real time.

What we have now on our sales team is real time access by a salesperson to everything they need to know to manage their business. Before computer-enabled sales calls, our salespeople would walk in the door of pharmacies and spend the first fifteen minutes to one hour responding to complaints: "Did you know that my order two days ago is missing two bottles of…?" and on and on. It was totally reactive. Because pharmacists are very busy, all our people had time for, after all that, was two minutes to say, "Hey, we've got a new deal...." Now they walk in and say, "Sorry that bottle was missing the other day. That will never happen again. By the way, we cleared that credit issue, that return you sent in." And the customer's blown away. A lot of the sales force had to be replaced as we went through this change because if you've been around twenty years and are used to the reactive mode it's sometimes hard to go proactive.

We've got a Webmaster now. We've got a head of Internet processing and intranet processing. The whole approach is to find a way for businesspeople to be dragged screaming down the hall, "I need to have this!"

---

the sort of "bottom-up" revolution that brought swarms of personal computers into companies nearly two decades ago. Already, young, Web-savvy software engineers and managers in slow-moving big companies are writing programs in the Web's HTML language, and they are even using these programs to create new, easier-to-use front ends for retrieving data from the corporate mainframe computers. They are ignoring aging official company software and beginning to do their jobs with the help of brand new (and free) applications programs downloaded from the Net, like those in Netscape's Applications Foundry, for everything from human resources to financial management (www.netscape.com). Many are using unfinished applications programs—prototypes riddled with bugs—having come to the correct conclusion that given the wildly accelerating pace of change, a polished, bug-free software product is likely to be a polished, bug-free, *obsolete* software product.

As much as this Web-inspired insurrection is helping employees to streamline their particular tasks, it is also causing the sort of operational chaos that the PC infiltration did. But then chaos attends all new beginnings, all births, all genuine creativity and innovation. The advent of the real time corporation is no exception to this rule.

The real time message:

The task of implementing a real time corporation is difficult and complex, but it is an essential investment in your competitive future. The implementation of real time systems will have the effect of changing the working relationships within your organization as well as those with your partners and customers. The application of the technology will change your corporate culture. As these systems are adopted, new ideas for services and products, new ways of gaining customer loyalty, and new methods of team collaboration will take shape. Then information technology will indeed become a valued corporate asset.

When new ideas are invented, diffused and are adopted or rejected, leading to certain consequences, social change occurs.

—EVERETT ROGERS, *Diffusion of Innovations*, 1962

In twenty years computer scientists have gone from speaking in terms of milliseconds (thousands of a second)

6 Continuous Discontinuous Change

to nanoseconds (billions of a second)—a compression of time almost beyond our powers to imagine. It is as though a person's entire working life of, say 80,000 paid hours—2,000 hours per year for forty years—could be crunched into a mere 4.8 minutes.

—ALVIN TOFFLER, *The Third Wave*, 1980

THE TRANSITION TO real time operation has begun to churn up huge creative chaos inside corporations—and this has its counterpart on the outside. In business in general, as in society at large, the run-up to the millennium is being marked by acute discontinuities in trends. On the inside of their organizations, managers operating at warp speed will come to understand the operational non sequitur as norm. On the outside—the business environment as a whole—they will experience jarring, large-scale shifts in perspective, orientation, and practice. Managers' ability to understand and adapt to these five kinds of discontinuity will be essential for success in their organizations in the age of real time:

1. From economies of scale to economies of time

2. From broadcast to access, or monologue to dialogue

3. From data content to people content

4. From fixed boundaries to open space

5. From the satisfied to the self-satisfied consumer

From Economies of Scale to Economies of Time

The noted physicist Freeman Dyson advises, "Never sacrifice economies of time for economies of size."[1] That is an idea with crucial implications for business today.

For the past quarter-century, driven on the one hand by advancing technology and on the other by intensifying competition, business has been compressing design, manufacturing, and distribution times. Technology serves the insatiable appetite for speed in innovation, productivity improvement, and cost cutting. No company even halfway attentive to its market is allowed to forget that speed is value. Consumers have grown to like speed. As I said in chapter 1, the shopping center, grocery store, TV, computer, workplace, and neighborhood have served as subliminal classrooms, educating consumers to demand satisfaction—now. Technology is what helps winners to get to market first, and the tools of time compression span a vast range—from FedEx delivery and ATMs to hand-held inventory scanners and on-line distribution centers. A global real time communications infrastructure with satellites as its principal building blocks is emerging as the technological key to acceleration in the future.

Hewlett Packard (www.hp.com), one of the world's leading suppliers of computer products and information systems, a $40 billion company growing at slightly more than 20 percent per year, supplies valuable clues to how business will profit from all of this. Joel Birnbaum is a senior vice president of R&D for the company and director of HP Labs. He told me:

> We're very much driven by time to market, and it's forced us to run our business quite differently....We seldom have the luxury of reassembling the teams to all be in the same place or even in the same country. Product development often involves combinations of divisions from France to California and elsewhere. Even so-called simple products like our InkJet printers require global teams. So we've had to learn how to work at a distance.

We have been using TCP/IP [Internet data communications protocols] since 1983, when I installed the first networks and the first VAX machine[2] in HP Labs. There was no rule against buying a competitor's product, but people said to me, "Gosh, right near Dave Packard's office you're going to put in a DEC-10 and a couple of VAXes!" I told Dave why these were needed and the advantages of collaboration on design around the world, and he agreed.

I also told him, "One of these days we'll have a bonfire in the parking lot and we'll burn all the VAXes as soon as we have the horsepower to replace them with our own machines." Actually, we could have done that a few years ago.

That was the beginning of our connecting servers to distributed design operations using TCP/IP. Today, our internal Internet traffic exceeds 7 to 8 trillion bytes per month. We send about 1.6 million e-mails a day on TCP/IP networks inside the organization. We have 130,000 computer hosts around the world serving 112,000 employees.

In a business where 77 per cent of our revenue comes from products introduced in the past two years, we see real time communication and collaboration as a competitive asset.[3]

Hewlett Packard has helped shape the modus operandi of Silicon Valley, where companies are always on the edge of the future, making it happen rather than drafting elaborate prognostications about it. Growth forecasts, such as five- and ten-year projections for product sales, are routinely ignored because they are seen as mere extrapolations from history. Instead, people are in constant touch with the technological and competitive environment of the moment. Change is treated as an opportunity that, if spotted ahead of competitors and acted on as fast as possible, can transform the ranking of companies in an industry virtually overnight. The advantages of (industry) leadership can vanish in a flash. Decisions are made in tight, collaborative networks, and mistakes corrected as fast as they are spotted. "Speed is our differentiation," says Mike Homer, the vice president of Netscape.

Speed does not allow for much planning—or for the leisurely deployment of decision-making tools such as opinion polls, surveys, and focus groups, on which managers once relied for security and a sense of direction. The improvisational Silicon Valley style of management is perfectly adapted to the chaotic changes characteristic of transitional eras like this one. Silicon Valley also supplies the clearest examples of the penalties paid for delayed reaction.

In February 1996, for instance, I met with Gil Amelio, newly appointed chief executive of Apple Computer (www.apple.com), on his second day with the company. I volunteered my recommendations for reversing Apple's declining fortunes—among them, to get operating costs down, to outsource manufacturing, to license Java, and to work on rebuilding relationships with third-party software developers. Above all, I said, he must act *quickly* to implement a shortlist of critical changes within the first quarter of his watch. Patience is not a characteristic of today's marketplace. He shook his head, insisting that the turnaround would take three years. One year after he took over, both Apple's share of the personal computer market and its stock price had declined 40 percent, and software developers were abandoning the Macintosh platform in droves. Without prompt evidence of his intention to effect sweeping changes at the company's core, the world outside Apple lost confidence in its prospects, in a widening ripple effect.

Like forces of nature or "acts of God," technological and market forces move so rapidly, and the warning signs of change are so subtle, that managers more often than not fail to see them— or their effects—coming. Porsche lost 80 percent of its U.S. market share in just five years in the early 1990s. In 1995, an unscrupulous young trader making unsanctioned, derivative investments from his computer console in Singapore brought about the fall of Barings, the hundred-year-old British financial institution. Only one-third of the companies on the Fortune 500 list at midcentury still survive today; more than half of the top twenty computer companies in the United States were not in business twenty years ago. Now, as time flies, much that is familiar and seemingly rock solid flies out the window with it.

> ## As time flies, much that is familiar and seemingly rock solid flies out the window with it.

Everywhere today, the change-resistant are rapidly taught the error of their ways. John Akers, the erstwhile chairman and chief executive officer of IBM (www.ibm.com), had planned a strategic redirection of the company in 1993. But in the wake of several quarters of sliding revenue growth and years of declining competitive standing, Wall Street and powerful institutional investors did not give him the chance to implement his ideas. As a result of his relative tardiness in plotting his reorganization, he was forced out of his job within months of his plan's conception.

From Broadcast to Access, or Monologue to Dialogue

Broadcast means the dissemination of the same information to everyone in predigested form; *access* means that consumers choose what information they want, where and when they want it, and in what form. As we move closer to a real time world, the term *access* will have widening application, going beyond the confines of ready provision of mere information to the delivery of products and services.

The old adage of "location, location, location" being the three most important advantages in retailing now applies to almost every consumer-oriented service. While the Internet is the most technically sophisticated and extreme application of this idea, other developments are equally striking and tremendous in scope. It was not too many years ago when gas stations were the primary contender for the best locations in every big and small town. Now ATMs, fast food outlets, specialty coffee shops, and video rental stores seem to vie for space on every street corner.

Ubiquity is the order of the day. Blockbuster (www.block buster.com), the video rental chain, has 5,021 stores worldwide and is adding new ones at the rate of one every eleven hours. McDonald's, which had 11,803 restaurants worldwide in 1990, grew to 18,380 in 1995 (www.mcdonalds.com). Vendors of consumer electronics like Best Buy (www.bestbuy.com) and Circuit City (www.circuitcity.com) are opening new stores at the rate of 25 percent of their total outlets a quarter. People at Taco Bell refer to their 1,500-plus outlets as POA's, or points of access, or anyplace people eat: a supermarket, airport, school cafeteria, college campus, or street corner.[4]

Customers must have easy and quick access to satisfaction, whether they need help with a purchase, a reorder, a check on order status, or catalog information or want to air their frustrations. Businesses have gotten this message. Telephone companies are almost sold out of 800 numbers in the United States, with 97 percent of all currently available numbers in use. Whether the 800 numbers belong to Hershey's chocolates (1-800-468-1714), Kellogg's Raisin Bran (1-800-962-1413), Intuit's Quicken (1-800-4-INTUIT), or Dell Computers (1-800-624-9897), they offer service, value, and, above all, dialogue. Studies show that consumers believe 800 numbers on products connote quality inside.[5]

Use of an answering machine and taped reply message is not the way to deal with consumers. From dialogue, companies must build databases, respond to suggestions and criticism, and customize products or services. This is how the customer satisfaction loop for the never satisfied customer should be completed.

Access has a way of revitalizing old industries and businesses. One of the best examples is book publishing and bookstores. Kicking a bit of sand in Nicholas Negroponte's all-digital-world theory that books will vanish, Americans bought 1.5 billion books in 1995, an increase of more than 30 percent since 1991.[6] In the last decade, bookstores have popped up everywhere. Two of my favorite stores are tucked away in the small villages of Kona and Wailea on the island of Hawaii. Their new, computer-based inventory systems allow them to special-order from distributors in Honolulu or the mainland on-line, giving them the chance to hold their own against the large superstores and other competitors.

Access will revitalize old industries.

These rivals include the ultimate accessible bookstore, Amazon.com, an on-line operation that boasts an inventory of 2.5 million book titles (www.amazon.com). It's great to browse from home. I have an account billed to my credit card. The Amazon.com service department is helpful and responsive, replying by e-mail to address problems and notifying you when your order is being shipped. It also maintains a database on customer orders and informs you when your favorite author has published again. Amazon.com has one-upped Barnes & Noble (www.barnesandnoble.com). While I enjoy browsing and having a cup of cappuccino at the bookstore from time to time, I find the quick and easy access to Amazon.com saves me time. And I buy more books.

As we morph from the age of computing and information to the age of communications, technological progress is opening the door wide to a content-rich, multimedia dialogue. In 1985, the average personal computer contained 128 kilobytes of RAM memory and 256 kilobytes of hard-disk storage. Today the average personal computer has 32 megabytes of RAM and 1 gigabyte (1 billion bytes) of disk storage. To express this progression in more familiar terms, a personal computer, circa 1985, could store only 500 pages of text. Today, on my computer with a 1.2 gigabyte disk drive, I can store more than 7 million pages.

Now consider the same progression, only speeded up and applied to the bandwidth of communications. Increased bandwidth means more than greater speed of transmission and reception, it also means having the capacity to send and receive video images and sound in real time.

Because progress in expanding bandwidth (expressed in bits per second, or the rate at which bits flow through your telephone line or the cable to your TV) lags far behind the rate of advance in MIPS (millions of instructions per second, or the rate at which computers process data of any kind) our ability to replicate face-to-face interaction in its fullest dimensions through telephone, cable, or wireless communication is still quite primitive today. An average computer is capable of handling less than a minute of video. One megabyte of storage can hold only fifty spoken words, five photographs, and five seconds of video. But these capacities are about to change dramatically. In the early part of the twenty-first century, the communications infrastructure will begin to accommodate two-way dialogue in an interactive, television-like environment, at prices most consumers will be able to afford.

George Gilder, the most enthusiastic proponent of bandwidth expansion, vividly expresses the scope of the new revolution:

> Like the great river headed for a falls, a new factor of production is racing toward a historic cliff of costs. Over the next 30 years, the spearhead of wealth creation will be the telecosm, marked by the plummeting cost of bandwidth—communications power—measured in gigabits per second.[7]

I have already had more than a glimpse of this technological watershed. My home is slated to be a beta site for the @Home (www.home.net) joint venture with Tele-Communications, Inc., or TCI (www.tci.com), that allows access to the Internet via cable. This will increase my download speed to 10 megabytes per second (millions), a huge improvement over my "high-speed" ISDN line's capacity of only around 156 kilobytes (thousands) per second. I will be able to download a ninety-minute movie in about ten minutes versus four hours by ISDN, or two and a half *days* over my telephone line.

Video conferencing from living rooms and desktop computers with the clarity of high-definition television will make for more engaging conferences, team meetings, and exchanges of

Image Transmission Times in Different Data Systems

	Standard Phone Line Analog	ISDN Phone Line Digital	ASDL T-1	Cable
Simple still image, 2 megabits	2.3 minutes	35.7 seconds	1.3 seconds	0.5 seconds
Complex still image, 15 megabits	18.5 minutes	4.8 minutes	10.7 seconds	4 seconds
Short animated video, 72 megabits	1.4 hours	21.5 minutes	48 seconds	18 seconds
Long animated video, 4.3 gigabits	3.5 days	21.4 hours	48 minutes	18 minutes

Increases in bandwidth or capacity of the communicating medium will require improvements in various software techniques such as compression as well as the upgrading of the transmission technologies to real time.

Source: Forrester Research, Inc., Cambridge, MA. Reprinted with permission.

consumer feedback, and it will enhance the illusion of "being there" that television first created.

The technologies of acceleration in themselves are of little interest to the average consumer. But speed means bandwidth, and bandwidth means "dialogue"—which in turn also means more control and choice of content by consumers. It is interaction, something consumers love.

As I have shown in chapter 2, the dialogue that bandwidth makes possible allows consumers to satisfy many of their needs themselves. As a result—somewhat paradoxically—while consumers take more control over what and how they buy, they are, in another sense, more open to being influenced and guided by companies.

> Real time technologies will allow customers to satisfy many of their needs themselves.

From Data Content to People Content

Recent developments in technology such as the Internet are propelling advances in a panoply of delivery mechanisms and information services, including interactive TV and desktop video conferencing. What is the most important implication of all these new communications media that are digital, cheap, and bidirectional? Because they are digital, the various forms of media can be mixed and matched: video, voice, data, and graphics can all be combined into new forms for human interaction. And what this in turn means is that, just as the left and right brain work together to allow such complex and delicate experiences as "feeling," "enjoying," "understanding," and "trusting," the new media will permit infinitely more subtle communication and nuanced human interaction. It is this capacity for the exchange of complex human experience, rather than the hardware and software that now get so much attention, that will come to be associated with computer power.

Bandwidth expansion allows for a much fuller range of human expression. Information is, after all, something far richer than our conventional notion of it as data stored in computer warehouses. Visual and aural cues are part of it. But, going even further than that, we often forget that the most important aspect of information is the expression and acceptance of its meaning. It is a smile, a frown, a head shake, a hug, and a kiss. We may not get to the stage where computers can kiss, but they will certainly be able to mimic human emotions in a far more satisfying way. The closer technology comes to delivering the subtleties of human expression, the more we will come to rely on it for human interaction—in the marketplace as much as anywhere else.

You might say that as the bandwidth of expression expands, *people* become content: knowledge as well as graphic, intimate, even viscerally affecting human experiences will become the common currency of exchange and interaction.

From Fixed Boundaries to Open Space

A few years ago I heard an inventor named Paul MacCready speak on the subject of new ideas at the Technology Museum in San Jose. Best known as the father of human-powered flight, Mac-Cready, an American, won Britain's Kremer Prizes for two accomplishments: sustaining human-powered flight over a fixed course, and then across the English Channel, with the *Gossamer Condor* and *Gossamer Albatross*, both of which he designed and built himself. At the lecture I attended, he retold the story recounted in his book *The Flying Gossamer*[8] of how he won a prize of £50,000 for designing a flimsy aircraft made of balsa wood, paper, and other light materials. He had pulled off something that many of his aeronautical engineer colleagues and a variety of other specialists vying for the award had failed to accomplish. Nearly everything about MacCready's approach effectively threw out one hundred years of theory about aircraft design.

MacCready said he had entered the competition chiefly because he needed the money. He figured that all he had to do was make his craft as light as possible—an aim he accomplished in part by using his ten-year-old son as pilot—and keep the *Gossamer* airborne for just long enough to win. He gave no thought to accessories for his creation or to its looks, having decided that "it didn't even have to look like a plane." The *Gossamer* literally fell apart as it flew, but that worked to Mac-Cready's advantage, lightening the load on the craft as his son's pedaling power wound downward.

MacCready said that the lesson he learned was, "Someone else always determines how we think." In their design attempts, the other competitors had all gone by the book without ever once asking the question, "Why are we stuck on these rules?"

Certainly, with the exception of rare wild individuals like MacCready, few of us stand to profit from discounting the experience and understanding of those who have gone before us. Yet many theories, practices, and procedures become institutionalized. They are never challenged or questioned, and as a result they actually block ideas about new and better ways of doing things. Particularly in business, thinking is too often a captive of the past—of past leaders' approaches to everything from organizational structure to the importance accorded one or another management specialization to the way the outside world is viewed and tackled.

The modern organizational chart reflects management science's early twentieth-century fondness for boxes—strictly divided and segregated corporate functions and managerial disciplines, roles, and responsibilities. The walls between the boxes restrict the talents and contributions of the employees they enclose to particular spheres of operation. Within each box, employees' identities are a matter of rigid categorization by function, job description, and pay level. In government organizations, which perhaps most closely resemble the Orwellian nightmare of 1984, employees to this day describe themselves as "level 2 managers" or something similar.

The top-to-bottom overhaul in organizational practices instigated by the Japanese-inspired total quality management revolution taught managers about the drawbacks of boundaries and boxes. Quality, they learned, could not be the sole concern of a specialized department at the end of the line, a line beginning with the product development box and ending with the box marked "production." Quality had to become everyone's job; it had to be integrated into design, manufacturing, distribution, and service, which in turn meant that all of these managerial functions could not be operationally segregated. Jamshid Gharajedaghi, president and CEO of Interact, former director of the Busch Center, and adjunct professor of systems sciences at the Wharton School at the University of Pennsylvania (www.wharton.upenn.edu), reminds us that TQM has required managers to rethink organizational cultures:

> The organization is redesigned to create a new platform for effective interactions among the "purposeful" members of the organization. It is to produce a shared understanding and commitment to a collective vision of a desired future. By dissolving paralyzing conflicts, this vision empowers the members to pursue their desired ends and help them redefine, as needed, the operational targets.
>
> Redesign of the structure is to create a multidimensional network of internal and external producers, designers, and marketers for multiple utilization of the value chain and key competency. The multidimensional network can become a vehicle for sharing and managing the capacity within the system and its environment to minimize vulnerability.[9]

TQM, like real time, tears down the walls and boxes.

The coming of the Internet has added fresh impetus to managerial disaggregation. In one of the most striking illustrations of its possibilities, Paul Ambrose, a database software genius, set up his development company, Weblogic (www.weblogic.com), in his living room in 1995. He and a couple of friends developed a set of network software products that allow data to migrate easily between corporate databases and the Internet. When the group's first products were completed, beta versions were put up on the Net. No marketing or press releases whatsoever were issued. No sales force, no distributors, no retailers signed up in advance of launch. Within six weeks, Ambrose had more than a thousand corporate and government sites testing his programs. His users included people in financial services companies, health care, retailing, and consumer businesses based in Japan, the United Kingdom, and France as well as the United States. Without boundaries, Paul's homegrown business is booming.

Many job titles and time-honored functions within organizations are clearly changing, and some are destined to become extinct. Responsibilities are increasingly apt to overlap and clash: for instance, the roles of the CEO and the marketing VP often conflict. It becomes more and more difficult to say which of these managers should have a greater say in matters of a company's strategy, product direction, alliances and partnerships with other companies, and relations with Wall Street.

For organizations, incalculable benefits will come from collaborations or linkages between departments of design and manufacturing, of sales, distribution, and service, and of marketing and engineering. And all of these relationships will be intensified and refined by intranets; they will make for enhanced speed, improved economies, and toned competitive muscle.

Dave Packard, the legendary cofounder of Hewlett Packard,

once said that the development of new ideas is not limited by resources or technology but by another type of boundary—the limits of the imagination. But in its elevation lies the risk that creativity will be treated as a discrete process, just as quality control once was. Powerful and effective ideas are unlikely to emerge from isolating creativity on a pedestal. Instead, managers must learn to immerse themselves in their companies' actual circumstances, partly by using the information tools of the age of real time to constantly update the facts at their disposal, and partly by seeking as much direct contact as possible with customers, customers' customers, and the products and services of competitors. Creative thinking will arise naturally from a visceral sense of the state of things and from early intimations of new openings and opportunities—awareness acquired by an unbounded and active engagement with the environment.

Most business theories are too inward directed. More attention should be paid to external forces of change.

We do not yet know how to live in a boundary-free world. For roughly the past twenty years popular business theories have been based on corporate self-improvement. Organizations and their performance have been scrutinized, evaluated, and reshaped into leaner and more effective structures. Trends such as "managing by walking around," focusing on "core competencies," developing "value propositions," "entrepreneuring," "reengineering," and "down-sizing" all encourage a certain self-centered perspective in organizations. I do not want to imply that these approaches are necessarily wrong. I believe, however, that most business theorists and theories of the last quarter-century direct too much attention inward and too little to external forces of change.

Michael Porter may be one exception. In his book *The Competitive Advantage* he tells us:

> *Every industry has an underlying structure, or a set of fundamental economic and technical characteristics, that gives rise to competitive forces. The strategist, wanting to position his company to cope best with its industry environment or to influence that environment in the company's favor, must learn what makes the environment tick.*[10]

Knowing what makes an industry tick in a real time marketplace means keeping track of all the forces affecting it in real time.

From the Satisfied to the Self-Satisfied Consumer

The line separating products from services is rapidly disappearing. Marketers who build sturdy and enduring relationships with consumers act on the understanding that integral to successful product marketing is the establishment of an information-rich customer environment characterized by exceptional attentiveness, convenience, assurance, and comfort—in other words, service.

In the shift from products to services, specialized knowledge and human understanding rise to the forefront. Service has long been a person-to-person activity. What health care, financial services, consulting, dry cleaning, and auto repair and maintenance all have in common is that they require specific expertise and exchange of information—and that their valuation is generally a function of time.

Quality is related to both time and service. If, for example, my car is in the repair shop too often, I am well aware that I am losing time. If my health care provider forces me to change doctors, I must take the time to retell my medical history and establish a new relationship. Businesses have to address the frustration associated with lost time felt by consumers whose daily schedules are already jam packed. They must address it by *valuing their customers' time.*

Service, for the consumer, is "time value." When I receive a fax or send one, time is compressed. When I use an ATM or buy from a Lands' End (www.landsend.com) catalog, space is transformed. When a problem is solved quickly or a product replaced with no questions asked, the message I get is that *the consumer's time is valued.* Real time technology delivers an immediate service and transaction experience wherever I am. In a real time world, the shopping mall becomes as readily accessible as if I were actually there, the service representative as if he were at my elbow.

My firm is a service business. Earlier this year, I gave a presentation to one of our clients in Tokyo. Four members of my project team, including my partner, Hiroshi Menjo, who heads our Japan practice, had to remain in Palo Alto. Because Hiroshi understands the technology and had worked on the project, he and the team were able to participate in the presentation through teleconferencing. I made the presentation; Hiroshi translated for my audience in Tokyo. It wasn't perfect, but it turned out far better than any of us had imagined. We saved both our customers and ourselves time and, when questions arose, delivered the necessary expertise.

The cellular telephone, satellite communications, and convenience marketing have all been changing our perceptions of space so that this truth is only now dawning on us: owing to the apparent reconfiguration of time and space, products and services are not distinct but a part of a continuum, and the distinction between products and services will continue to erode as diversity, choice, and competition force producers to think differently about time, space, and service.

My favorite cartoon character, created by Cathy Guisewite, is her namesake, Cathy, who seems to have better insight into the nuances of the marketplace than most market research people I know. In the clip from her comic strip pictured here, Cathy tells us why we are so unhappy as consumers. All of the problems she mentions happen to be real time service opportunities for companies.

Thoughts on a Real Time World

Service is a speed and response business. Investing in the technologies of self-service is the way companies will collapse waiting time and create memorably congenial experiences of interaction for their customers. It is this, I believe, that will create lasting brand loyalty. An 800 phone number, fax number, and a URL on the product for phone, fax, or on-line registration are real time service and brand-building opportunities that would turn Cathy into a very happy consumer.

As I have shown in chapter 2, my definition of perfection in service is customers serving themselves so effortlessly—through "transparent" technological intermediaries—that they are hardly aware of doing so. The telephone industry made this switch many years ago. For fifty years telephone operators sat at switchboards, waiting on callers. In the 1930s, relay switching systems transferred that task to the person making the phone call. In the 1960s, push-button phones turned the caller into a computer operator by providing a computer keypad on the phone that allows calls and data to be directed to millions of possible receivers. To my knowledge, no one complained about having to become his or her own telephone operator. Today,

"Life in the '90s: All Warranties, No Satisfaction"

In this strip by Cathy Guisewite, her cartoon counterpart, Cathy, says:

"Electric toothbrush. Jammed after two months. Didn't take it back because I felt guilty that I might not have followed the instructions for proper maintenance exactly. Coffeemaker. Failed after six days. Couldn't return it to the manufacturer because I threw out the original packaging. Instant wrinkle steamer. Never worked at all. Couldn't demand a refund because if I had time to get a box, wrapping paper and a certified mail receipt, I wouldn't be the sort of person who needed an instant wrinkle steamer. Hairdryer. Broke after three weeks. Didn't send it back because I couldn't live for one day without one, and once I bought the new one I quit worrying about the old one. Nine-function cordless phone. Quit functioning. Couldn't get it fixed because I threw out the registration card, lost the receipt and forgot where I bought it. Defective answering machine. Couldn't return it because of the slight possibility that the defect was caused by me hurtling it across the room. Life in the '90s—all warranties, no satisfaction."

computers, software, and the networks turn everyone into researcher, publisher, order clerk, and bank teller.

For companies properly primed for the five kinds of discontinuity I have described in this chapter, each shift will seem like a booster rocket that—even as it jars the frames of corporate spacecraft and tests managers' nerves—will shoot them into galaxies of undreamed of opportunities.

The real time message:

Real time managers will be different from today's in five important ways: They will not sacrifice economies of time for economies of scale. They will understand that consumers given more control over what and how they buy through dialogue with companies are, paradoxically, consumers more open to being guided by companies. They will use—both inside and outside their companies—new media allowing unprecedentedly subtle and nuanced human interaction. They will have seen how real time tears down organizational walls and boxes, just like TQM. They will invest heavily in technologies that let customers satisfy themselves.

Creativity occurs in an act of encounter and it is to be understood with this encounter as its center.

—ROLLO MAY, *The Courage to Create*, 1975

Uncertainty—in the economy, society, politics—has become so great as to render futile, if not counterproductive, the kind of planning most companies still practice: forecasting based on probabilities.

—PETER DRUCKER, *Wall Street Journal*, July 22, 1992

7

Preparing for the Eventuality of Anything

THERE IS A single most common reaction from audiences I have been addressing about the age of real time. "Well," the very first person to raise a hand at question time is likely to say, "It's all fascinating, but what do we *do* about it?"

In the introduction to this book I mentioned Alvin Toffler's hope in writing *Future Shock* that his readers, being properly prepared for the technology-driven seismic jolts in store for us, would handle these disturbances more deftly than the uninstructed and unprepared. But if the nearly three decades since his book's debut have taught us anything, it is that managers of organizations cannot, in fact, prepare for the age of real time in the way they might for "driving a car down a crowded street, piloting a plane...or dealing with interpersonal difficulties." There are decades' worth of precedents for coping with problems of that sort, but practically none for what a successful transition to real time entails, which is, above all, *preparing for the eventuality of anything*. For most people it entails a profound change in attitude and the acquisition of a new set of habits.

A Primer for Real Time Management

The best metaphor for the right way to approach real time might be the modus operandi of the reigning star of the private (as opposed to government) weather forecasting business—the head of the meteorology department of Smith Barney's (www.smithbarney.com) commodity trading arm. What is clear from a detailed account of how this expert, Jon Davis, works, is that forecasting is a complete misnomer for what he actually does, which is to stay so closely attuned to every available computer readout and analysis from every data-gathering instrument—measuring, for instance, wind, barometric pressure, and temperature—that he does not predict the weather so much as virtually live on top of changing weather patterns. He even monitors data sources that his less successful competitors never fuss with. According to an article in the *New York Times*, "One arcane factor that Mr. Davis tracks, but few others bother to chart, is the wavelike patterns, over months, in air pressures at specific latitudes that help track changes in the jet stream."[1] Leaders in real time management will use all the tools at their disposal to achieve a similar, tireless monitoring of indicators of gestating patterns, crosscurrents, and undercurrents in technologies, markets, and industries. The balance of this section of the chapter comprises my answer to the question of what organizations should do to prime themselves for managing in the age of real time.

The leaders in real time management will constantly monitor even the most minute changes.

Expand Your Toolkit of Sensors

If you currently rely on toll-free telephone numbers for customer feedback, add a Web site at which your customers can refine and expand their dialogue with you. If you already have a Web site and an 800 number, add transaction capabilities to your real time data-gathering resources. Invest in and continually refine your human interface software, adding multimedia technologies and pushing the edges of bandwidth to entice your customers and employees and keep them engaged with entertaining interaction. Maintaining an interface of this sort is challenging and expensive, but you will be rewarded with intense involvement and nonstop information feedback. Most important, this compelling front-end interface must be tied into a database, a network, and feedback procedures.

As a kind of personal, informal investigation into how much progress companies have been making in this direction—and to satisfy my curiosity—I have developed a habit of calling 800 numbers I read on packages and in ads. Often, people on the other end of the phone seem surprised that the phone rang. I ask what they do with the information they get from callers, and they tell me: Nothing. In fact, the person on the other end of the phone gets defensive when I ask if the company intends to use the information from my call to build a database or give feedback to management.

Sources of Real Time Information

Real time information systems provide up-to-date information in a continuous flow, preparing management for the eventuality of anything.

This is misplaced and unwarranted defensiveness—as if the person on the other end of the line is afraid that an admission to collecting information amounts to an espousal of Big Brotherism. As I have shown in chapter 3, that fear is completely out of date. We have to find ways to communicate to our customers, and would-be customers, that any information they supply us with is intended to help us better respond to their needs.

One notion of the shape of things to come is suggested by Cybergold (www.cybergold.com), a Silicon Valley start-up taking an all-electronic approach to advertising. It pays Net surfers to read about a company's products and services and to supply demographic data and answers to questions about their interests and preferences. The surfing consumer is given an account, which accumulates cyberbucks that can be traded for cash, products, or services. But Net shoppers get more than that: they are only asked to read about products and services that Cybergold matches to their stated needs or wants. Information is, in effect, traded for information.

As a company accumulates such data, it will be able to use data-mining techniques to develop detailed perspectives on customers' actions and buying patterns—invaluable aids to designing products and services for them.

Take a Lead from "Good Science"

Rapid and continuous adjustment based on regular sampling is the key to success in any fast-changing environment or field of study. It is essentially the same approach that the physicist Freeman Dyson has advocated in the interests of "good science" in the exploration of space. New discoveries, he argues, can change the questions that science asks—the priorities of scientific research—practically overnight. Hence, "the tools of science should be versatile and flexible"—or quite the opposite of the big space missions, whose plans are set in concrete years in advance and are thus out of date by the time of launch, having been designed to answer questions for which no one now wants or needs answers. Far preferable to expensive, major missions, Dyson says, are frequent and relatively cheap small missions.

> *If we want to investigate seriously the question of life on Mars, the best way would be to plan a regular series of Mars missions…so that we could learn from the results of one mission the right questions for the next mission to ask. We could also learn from the mistakes of one mission how to avoid mistakes on the next. In almost any field of space science, whether we are exploring planets or galaxies or our own Earth, a series of modest missions is more likely than a single big spectacular to produce important discoveries.* [2]

Think Software

In the twenty-first century, software will be one of the most vital assets of any real time corporation—on a par with a company's distribution system and R&D. Although in this book I have particularly emphasized communications software—the nervous system of a real time infrastructure—it is not only the lightning-paced exchange of data that accounts for software's increasingly important position in the corporation. Software allows companies to reshape the very nature of their business.

According to Jack Welch, the far-sighted leader of the General Electric Corporation (www.ge.com),

> *GE's goal is not to become smaller but to get the small-company soul and small-company speed inside our big-company body.* [3]

It is the standardization yet flexibility of software that, more and more, is allowing even massive enterprises like GE to match the reflexes, adaptability, and intimacy of small shops closely in touch with their customers. Because software allows tighter collaboration and synchronization of all the spheres of a company's operations, every mission-critical bit of shared knowledge can play a galvanizing role across the network, joining everyone from the backroom researcher, designer, and production line supervisor to the salesperson, the service manager, supplier, partner, and customer. The unprecedentedly efficient marketplace resulting from this will, ultimately, be the creation of software—the most powerful of those transparent agents already affecting all of us.

Learn by Doing

Because there are neither signposts nor established paths to real time management, organizations can really do no more than grope their way toward it. Every day, they grapple with the unknown—what-is-yet-to-be—much like an artist facing a blank canvas. This groping is ground zero for all creative enterprises and, as the psychologist Rollo May has observed, artists only discover what they can and should be doing by encountering or immersing themselves in their subjects. Would-be leaders of real time organizations learn by doing. They take a calculated risk and act on what they do know, even when that little is far outweighed by all that they don't know about the appropriateness or consequences of their actions. They learn to gauge what they should try next from the smallest shift in the wind. As noted by Kim Polese, the former Sun manager in charge of marketing for Java, an entire strategy can be reoriented in the blink of any eye.

Implementing the technologies of real time is the best and only guide to their likely evolution and significance—advice that my old friend Steve Jobs, cofounder of Apple, NeXT, and Pixar, both gives and takes himself. Start *somewhere*: this is what I call the "beachhead" approach to cultural change. Think small. Something as trivial seeming as putting all employees on an

Thoughts from Real Time Warriors
Kim Polese of Marimba, Inc. (www.marimba.com)

Kim Polese is the thirty-five-year-old president of Marimba, a Silicon Valley software company founded in 1996 to mine the potential of the Internet-oriented software product Java. Marimba demonstrates ways in which the Valley is the crucible for the real time world to come. Here, companies turn not on a dime but on a pixel. They can and do redesign their corporate strategies when their supersensitive sensors carry the first hint of a change in trends. Marimba shows how much thought and effort is going into finding ways of personalizing products, anticipating that personalization will be the norm in the age of real time. And Kim Polese, like just about everyone else, reports an acute personal awareness of the compression of time.

I was blown away the first time I saw Java. I was, at that time, the product manager for C++ at Sun Microsystems. I understood what the limitations of software development were and the big hurdles that existed, and with one fell swoop, all of those problems went away. I'm talking about a programming language that allowed you to develop an application once and have it run on multiple platforms; that it didn't matter what the operating system was anymore.

So I fell in love with Java and knew I wanted to work with it. And at that time, it was aimed at the consumer market—at personal digital assistants and set-top boxes. But only a few months after I got there, I and the chief technical officer of the company ended up writing a plan that said, we need to start pointing at the desktop, we need to aim at the information superhighway. The desktop, on-line services, the Internet, were just beginning to come into people's consciousness.

Getting to the point where the company actually did realign in that direction was a difficult task, and it was frustrating at times. But within six months, the team was able to complete a 180-degree turn and remake this programming language into Java, the Internet-based technology. We hit it right in terms of the timing, and it was incredible. Java was dynamic and was really about bringing the Internet to life and enabling bits of code to fly around and land on computers and perform interesting actions. Turn the Internet into a dynamic environment, a responsive environment, rather than a static, text-based environment.

The Java vision is continuing in Marimba and is driving our business and our technology decisions today. Six years ago, back at Sun Microsystems, when Java was originally conceived, the belief was that people should not have to deal with technology. We've all become so accustomed to having to install software and worry about what the underlying operating system is. It's as if every time you wanted to watch your TV, you needed to install some special device. Imagine if you had to buy a different TV for a different sitcom. That's what people have to put up with today in the computer market, for example, when they have to choose between a Macintosh and a Windows computer, based on what application each will run. Software should install itself and run. Software upgrades should happen again just as magically—they should happen across the network.

So, Castanet, the product that is really the focus of Marimba, is basically designed to automatically deliver programs to your desktop or whatever your device happens to be, and then enable them to update themselves intelligently in the background. You can think of Castanet as an automatic delivery system for software applications and content. You can think of it as turning static applications into live, automatically delivered channels, like channels on your television, like channels on your cable system.

One of the key aspects of this is personalization—the ability to know who the person is that you're delivering this application to, and to know their likes and dislikes and their preferences. One application would be—imagine Charles Schwab, imagine being able to basically monitor your stock portfolio with a very friendly user interface, and not just monitor it, but have Schwab suggest, perhaps, stocks that you might be interested in, based on information trends you've been following over the last couple of years. Or you might want to try sophisticated "what-if?" scenarios about market conditions and whether you're going to sell something short based on where the market is today, at this point and time during the day, and based on your total portfolio. You get an ability to customize, to personalize: I am the customer, and Schwab knows who I am and what I like to invest in.

And to update the software on an ongoing basis, the tuner, the transmitter, basically polls for an update. Silently, in the background—so that the user is not aware of it—it asks, "Is there an update?" And that can happen every minute or every hour or overnight. The frequency can be set by Schwab, but the consumer can override it if they don't want to have their modem going off every fifteen minutes. They can choose frequent, hot updates, or say, "Well, I only want this thing to update between four and six in the morning." That's something people can adjust to their needs.

Another example might be a catalogue, an L. L. Bean type of company that knows which designer I like, knows my waist size, knows what colors look good on me, and therefore suggests various pieces of clothing based on that, or tells me about the sale of the day. Knows my purchasing pattern. Knows that I typically go on a shopping spree right before Christmas, or whatever it happens to be.

This is what we want—technology working for people rather than people working for technology.

We built the company and got a product out in the marketplace in less than eight months. It seems strange. I think back to an event that happened and think, oh yeah, that was a couple of years ago. Then I realize that it was really about six months ago! When I think of the weird tricks time has been playing just in the last couple of years, it's so odd, and it has been accelerating just in the last few years. Everybody is speeding toward adopting the new technologies because they see the potential for services and products.

And we're working our butts off! We're packing two days into one day every day. I don't think I've ever left here at two or three in the morning and not had a few other people who are here working, too. We live here. It turns out that that fits in very well with my personality. I've always been the kind of person that completely and utterly throws myself into something. And the best part is—we're having a bash. Being a part of a start-up right here in Silicon Valley is an incredibly intense but exciting experience. I wouldn't want to be doing anything else.

e-mail network can become a powerful hidden agent of change (see chapter 5). Spend enough money and time so that that one application and one example are successful. Use incentive systems to drive your organizational culture forward. Reward people for communicating and sharing information, for building databases that give consumers greater access, for telecommuting. Give people computers to work on at home—to interact with one another, service customers, answer e-mail.

And don't let yourself be paralyzed by fear of failure. Remind all employees that in Silicon Valley, part of the legend of the microchip champion, Intel, is the stream of losing products the company put out in the 1980s. Intel kept moving, learning from its errors, treating each failure as if it were one of Freeman Dyson's minimissions to outerspace.

Thoughts from Real Time Warriors

Steve Jobs, Cofounder of Apple, NeXT, and Pixar Animation Studios (www.pixar.com)

The cofounder of Apple, NeXT, and Pixar, now chairman and CEO of Pixar Animation Studios, talked to me about how rapidly technological progress outdates yesterday's miracles; about ways in which technology warps our sense of scale and dimensions; about the open and receptive state of mind that is the essential prerequisite for breakthrough creativity. It might surprise some readers to learn that Steve Jobs, like almost all great technology pioneers and enthusiasts, is by no means immune from anxiety about technology's potential to do harm. He began our conversation with a look back at his first personal computer and its place in history.

The Apple II's appeal was that it was the binary pioneer. It was the machine that brought people from darkness to light, so to speak, so you didn't argue about how bright the bulb was. If you were in New York in 1896, reading by the light of your first light bulb instead of a candle, you didn't think, "Well, in twenty years the light bulbs are going to be a lot brighter." When you go from zero to one, that is a greater percentage increase than from one to anything else. It's an infinite percent increase, and that's what the Apple II was. In my perspective, it was a greater leap than any subsequent leap.

• • • •

Technology cuts both ways. It's a double-edged sword. Several years ago, I got a T1 (a high-capacity digital communications link) from the company to my house because I guessed that everyone was going to have a T1 to their house one day soon and that I should be an early adopter and experience what it's like. Maybe I could learn something early and guide some of our products to take advantage of it. So, with this very high bandwidth to my home in place, people can send me e-mail over the Internet and I receive it instantly.

What this means is that they learn very quickly that, if I want to, I can respond immediately, even if I'm sitting at my computer at home at midnight. But this also means that if I don't respond instantly, there's no cover for me to hide behind. They expect it of me now. So, at nine o'clock at night, when I'm with my family, it's very hard to resist the urge to take fifteen minutes and go check my e-mail. It has really invaded my personal life, I have to say. It follows me everywhere—there's no escape anymore. Being connected is a wonderful thing, but being disconnected is a wonderful thing too. Like the place I go on vacation has, basically, no phones, no radios, no televisions, no computers. If you use a personal computer on the beach they ask you to put it away, because they don't want their other guests to have to deal with seeing it. There's nothing of the modern world there.

Work is not just for eight hours a day now—it just doesn't stop. I'm running two companies. It sounds like I'm a little frazzled, but I don't think I'm that unusual. When I get up in the morning, the first thing I do, after I see my kids, is to find a reason to go downstairs and check my e-mail, stock prices, and the like. Probably the last thing I do before I go to bed at night is check my e-mail. Pretty soon, there's going to be this little thing on my toes that will pull them till I wake up, if I get an important e-mail! I'm not saying all this is good or bad. We're still learning, and this idea of people all becoming knowledge workers is wonderful, but what does it mean for their kids?

• • • •

If you work really hard in technology, and you have a product that's a hit for a year or two, that's a big deal. If you have one that's a hit for five years, it's remarkable, very unique. If you hit the grandest slam of all time, you have one that's good for ten or fifteen years, like an Apple II or a Mac. But sooner or later, it becomes the sediment layer.

I actually find it incredibly useful to look at the world today, to experience the world today, as if I was just born into it. One of the things I've learned from every real artist is, if you want to stay an artist, you have to forget your past and just live as much in the moment as you can, and see things fresh, like if you were twenty. Otherwise, the color of your glasses gets so strong that you stop seeing things as they are, you see them through the color of your experience too much, and it's very difficult to do new things when your glasses get too colored.

I don't look at a computer and think, "Jeez, we made the first one of those twenty years ago, wow!" I want to look at it as only a computer, no big deal, only as 110 volts coming out of the wall. Because I'm sure there are people who were around for the Rural Electrification Act in the '30s, or whenever, who will tell you, even today, how incredible it is that you have 110 volts in your house. And they'll be right. But I've never lived in a house without 110 volts in it, and I don't think about it. I don't want to think about it, miraculous as it is, because if you do, you distract yourself from seeing things fresh. Which, I think, is how you do the next miraculous thing.

The Inside Service Network

Unfortunately, in most organizations, we still view service as fixing things after the fact. To build a real time culture, the different segments of organizations must learn to serve each other's needs proactively, just as they must learn to do for (outside) customers. To this end, tools such as databases and intranet browsers to search them can be acquired and put to work now. So, for instance, in real time, a salesperson in a large corporation making a bid on a big project in Tokyo should be able to order a search within his own organization back in Peoria for expertise he lacks and for missing pieces of the solution. He should be able to notify a sales manager in Hong Kong of key influences on the Tokyo customer's decision that happen to be located in her territory and enlist her help. He should be able to access the office of his corporation's president to see if the president can make a trip to Japan to close the deal.

Openness to exciting new ideas, along with a willingness to implement them, elicits from employees the sort of wild, round-the-clock dedication famously advertised on T-shirts worn by members of an Apple development team in the mid-80s: "Ninety Hours a Week and Loving It."

The Ever-Evasive Future

More than a decade ago, the Conference Board (www.conference-board.org) surveyed chief executive officers running large companies in the United States, Europe, Canada, and Latin America. A major finding of the study was that these corporate chieftains believed "the future of their businesses [would] be significantly different from the past, and in ultimately unpredictable ways." What the report said then is even truer today:

> In this environment, management, anxious to anticipate as many surprises as they can, probably produce more short-term and long-term forecasts on more subjects than ever before. But there is not much confidence in the result, and these forecasts are given limited credence as a basis for business and management action. Of course, competition, turbulence, and unpredictability have always been prominent features of the business scene...however...these themes have become sufficiently strong in top-management thinking to dominate strategies and shape management emphasis.[4]

The exciting challenge confronting managers is to soar, in a spirit of adventure, toward a horizon that may take just about any shape or form.

Real time message:

Companies will learn about the technologies of real time in the only way they truly can—by adopting them and putting them to practical use. They will deploy them not to predict the future but to live virtually on top of changing patterns and trends affecting every sphere of their business environment, making rapid and continuous refinements in their way of doing business.

EPILOGUE

The hype about productivity has been much greater than the performance. Maybe we have gotten so good at hype that the information revolution seems to us bigger than the electric motor seemed when it was invented. But the electric motor had a big impact on how many shirts you could sew in a day.

—ROBERT SOLOW, winner of the 1987 Nobel Prize in economics, 1996

"There's no use trying...one can't believe impossible things...."

"I daresay you haven't had much practice," said the Queen. "When I was your age, I always did it for half-an-hour a day. Why, sometimes I've believed as many as six impossible things before breakfast."

—LEWIS CARROLL, *Through the Looking-Glass, and What Alice Found There*, 1872

THERE ARE TIMES when we in the high-technology community feel a little defensive. When, for instance, some guru or other jumps on a soapbox to proclaim that computers have failed to live up to the expectation that they would boost productivity more dramatically than any other twentieth-century invention—and that they probably never will. Listening to this sort of thing, we feel a bit like Galileo's ghost, who had to wait three-and-a-half centuries to hear the Vatican concede—in 1992—that the earth is not a fixed body but revolves around the sun.

The story told by the official numbers from the Bureau of Labor Statistics, Productivity, and Testing is that productivity growth has slowed since the early 1970s. The numbers suggest that in service industries, productivity growth has declined sharply. Yet over this same period, American businesses have invested a steadily increasing share of their new capital equipment dollars in information technology. Economists discussing the technology's failure to affect productivity in the way everybody thought it would refer to the problem as "the productivity paradox."

In the debate over this puzzle, careful thinkers have suggested that the yardsticks are the problem—that conventional measures of productivity cannot come to grips with the kinds of value that information technology has been adding to industry. In fact, applying these yardsticks to businesses transformed by computer and communications technologies may not only underestimate the positive contributions of these tools but also produce absurd results. "To the extent that ATMs lead to fewer checks being written," Erik Brynjolfsson at MIT's Sloan School of Management (http://web.mit.edu/sloan/www) points out, "they can actually lower productivity statistics." He also notes that

> [T]he sorts of benefits ascribed by managers to information technology—increased quality, variety, customer service, speed, and responsiveness—are precisely the aspects of output measurement that are poorly accounted for in productivity statistics as well as in most firms' accounting numbers....The measurement problems are particularly acute for information technology use in the service sector and among white collar workers.[1]

We don't know how to live in a real time, boundaryless world. We will have to learn.

Among the other good explanations for the so-called paradox is that new technologies, before they can deliver their promise, often require an extended phase of learning by those who use them and those who sell them. The horrors of the present transitional phase are well illustrated by the Internal Revenue Service's attempt at computerization, described in the *New York Times* in early 1997:

> The Internal Revenue Service... [has] ...spent $4 billion developing modern computer systems that... "do not work in the real world."...Arthur Gross, an Assistant Commissioner of Internal Revenue who was appointed 10 months ago to rescue the agency's efforts, said customer service representatives must

use as many as nine different computer terminals, each of which connects to several different data bases, to resolve problems.... The failure of the modernization effort will mean years of frustration for taxpayers who get into a dispute with the I.R.S., especially one that involves records kept on two or more of its computer systems.... As the I.R.S. starts over, Mr. Gross said, it must abandon the "big bang" theory of integrating all of its own computers at once, and instead improve operations piecemeal.[2]

Such staggering adaptations and adjustments in the behavior of many institutions and individuals have to accompany the exploitation of technology, and there is usually a time lag before the payoff. Twenty years had to pass before the electrification of factories yielded striking productivity gains. In those two decades, the portability of electricity made it possible to build factories in locations chosen to maximize work-flow efficiency. Before the advent of electric power, factories could be constructed only where waterwheels, steam engines, and power-transmitting shafts and rods were close by.

Far from there being a productivity paradox, the problem may simply be that economists, statisticians, and others whose job it is to monitor changes in productivity are just as impatient as the rest of us. Conditioned by the technologies of real time, they expect that these tools will themselves demonstrate their full potential in real time. And that could well be the greatest irony of the age.

The Agony of Defeat

In the course of researching and writing this book, I have found little in American life to be immune from real time conditioning. Not even football games and football teams.

Growing up as a boy in Pittsburgh, I, like everyone else I knew, was a devoted fan of the Steelers. It made no difference to us that the home team only made the playoffs once between 1933, the year it was formed (as the Pittsburgh Pirates), and 1971, a stretch of nearly four decades, before it became one of the top NFL teams of the 1970s. And I honestly cannot remember a single instance in those years of a coach—or anyone else, for that matter—being blamed and then fired for the team's failure to win the National Championship. Expectations are quite the contrary today. In January 1997, San Francisco 49ers coach George Siefert—who has a longer string of percentage victories to his name than any other coach in the history of the NFL—was virtually fired after the team lost the Western Division Championship. In 1994, of the five teams that make up the National Football Conference East, the Redskins, Cardinals, and Cowboys all had first-year coaches. The New York Giants had a second-year coach, and the Eagles had one who had actually lasted four years. Owners of football teams now want coaches to achieve greatness in a single season, if not one game.

Who Would Have Thought...?

We are all getting used to a steady diet of strange and impossible things—from the global to the political to the intimately domestic.

Who would have thought that the late 1990s would find Walter Wriston, the former chairman and CEO of Citicorp, talking about an "information standard" (as opposed to, say, a gold standard) and "stateless money" in global currency markets:

Technology has overwhelmed public policy....What annoys governments about stateless money is that it functions as a plebiscite on your policy.... Today, if the president goes in the Rose Garden and says something dumb, the cross rate of the dollar will change within 60 seconds. This creates what I call the information standard. The information standard is more draconian than the gold standard, because the government has lost control of the marketplace.[3]

Who would have thought that as of only a few months ago I could call the 800 number of a financial software supplier for help with installation to receive instructions from a proficient technician whose baby was crying in the background. There this technician was in her home, somewhere in the United States, taking care of her newborn child, walking around and talking about the solution to my problem over her phone headset.

Who would have thought when I started my consulting firm in 1970 that in 1997 I could say that I know we are doing well when all the offices are empty. We give our employees powerful portable computers with high-speed modems that allow them to stay in close touch with each other whether they are in a client's office, on the road, or at home.

Who would have thought that technology would be responsible for reuniting families during the workday—after the industrial revolution drove them first out of farms and then down miles and miles freeways, often in divergent directions? Who would have thought that a day would come when my three-year-old granddaughter would live next door and stop by my home office to play on the computer next to mine, to watch me talk on my business phone, surf the Internet, send a fax, copy or print out a document, read and compose e-mail and a book?

I think I would have found it a lot easier to believe that in 1996 race car drivers would tear across a dry lake in northwestern Nevada in a competition to break the sound barrier—at 760 miles an hour.[4] After all, the first official land speed record, set in 1898 by one Gaston de Chasseloup-Laubat hurtling along at 24.5 miles an hour, had already been broken at least two dozen times by my tenth birthday. It is not technological progress so much as its effects that astound and rivet us now.

What all of this means is that in doing business amidst the blizzard of change that will characterize the twenty-first century, an attitude of openness and a willingness to explore and take risks will be essential to perceiving opportunities to leverage the special and particular competitive advantages of any one company. Winning organizations will be run in the expectation of relentless shifts and readjustments in the marketplace, in customers' expectations, and in the behavior of competitors. Like Lewis Carroll's Queen, they will anticipate surprises six times a day before breakfast. With the unpredictable, the unexpected, and the impossible making up the stuff of everyday life, a real time culture will be a corporate asset infinitely more valuable than the most intricate research and planning. That culture will be founded on a new interrelation between companies and customers created by the capacity of fully integrated real time systems for acute sensing, for dialogue, and for responsiveness, systems in touch with the marketplace twenty-four hours a day. And that is how managers will cope with the outstanding feature of the age of the real time consumer: the eventuality of anything.

Appendix: Web Sites

The following Web addresses reference the various companies and organizations I mention throughout the book. In addition, I have listed various sites I used for reading and research on the topic of real time.

ABC, www.abctelevision.com
Advertising Age, www.adage.com
Amazon.com, www.amazon.com
America Online, www.aol.com
American Express, www.americanexpress.com
American Society for Quality Control, www.asqc.org
Apple Computer, www.apple.com
@Home, www.home.net
AT&T Wireless Services, www.attws.com

Bank of America, www.bankamerica.com
Barnes & Noble, www.barnesandnoble.com
BBN, www.bbn.com
Best Buy, www.bestbuy.com
Blockbuster Entertainment, www.blockbuster.com
Burton Snowboards, www.burton.com
Business Week, www.businessweek.com

Caresoft, www.caresite.com
CBS, www.cbs.com
Century 21 Real Estate, www.c21realty.com
Circuit City, www.circuitcity.com
Citibank, www.citibank.com
Citicorp, www.citicorp.com

Civil War photographs, Smithsonian Institute,
    Washington, D.C., http://lcweb.loc.gov/rr/print
CNN, www.cnn.com
Coca-Cola, www.cocacola.com
Computerworld, www.computerworld.com/home
Conference Board, www.conference-board.org
Consumer Information Center, www.pueblo.gsa.gov
Consumer Reports, www.consumer.org
The Custom Foot, www.thecustomfoot.com
Cybergold, www.cybergold.com

Daimler-Benz, www.daimler-benz.com
Dell Computer, www.dell.com
Dole Foods, www.dole5aday.com
Dorritos, www.fritolay.com

Earthquake Research Institute, University of Tokyo,
    www.eri.u-tokyo.ac.jp
East Africa weather pattern, www.comet.net/Weather/climate/
    owl_africa_climate.html-ssi
Economist, www.economist.com
Endocrine Metabolic Medical Center (EMMC),
    www.diabeteswell.com

Fast Company, www.fastcompany.com
Federal Express, www.fedex.com
Financial Times (London), www.FT.com
Fortune magazine, http://pathfinder.com/fortune
Free On-line Dictionary of Computing,
    www.instantweb.com/foldoc

General Electric Corporation, www.ge.com
General Motors, www.gm.com
Graham Technology, www.graham.com

Helsinki banks, www.tradepoint.fi/infolinks/bankfin.html
Hershey's Foods Corporation, www.hersheys.com
Hewlett-Packard, www.hp.com
Hyatt Hotels & Resorts, www.hyatt.com

IBM, www.ibm.com
Intel, www.Intel.com
Internal Revenue Service, www.irs.ustreas.gov
Intuit, www.Intuit.com

J. D. Power and Associates, www.JDPower.com
JCPenney, www.jcpenney.com

K-2 In-Line Skates, www.k2sports.com
Kellogg's Company, www.kelloggs.com
Kennametal, www.kennametal.com
Killer Loop sunglasses, www.killerloop.com

Levi Strauss, www.levi.com
Lithuania, http://neris.mii.lt
Lucile Salter Packard Children's Hospital,
    www-med.stanford.edu/lpch

Market Relations Group, www.marketrelations.com
Massachusetts Institute of Technology. *See* MIT
McDonald's, www.mcdonalds.com
McDonnell Douglas, www.mdc.com
McGill University (Montreal), www.mcgill.ca
McKenna Group, www.mckenna-group.com
McKesson Corp., www.McKesson.com
Microsoft, www.microsoft.com
MIT Media Lab, www.media.mit.edu
MIT Sloan School of Management,
    http://web.mit.edu/sloan/www

National Football League, (NFL). www.nfl.com
NBC, www.nbc.com
NETdelivery Corporation, www.netdelivery.com
Netscape, www.netscape.com
New York Times, www.nytimes.com
Nielsen Media Research, www.nielsen.com
Nordstrom, www.nordstrom.com

ParaGraph International, www.paragraph.com
Pathfinder Research, www.pathfinder-research.com
Pepsi, www.pepsi.com
PepsiCo, www.pepsico.com
Philips Electronics N.V., www.philips.com
Pier 1 Imports, www.pier1.com
Pillsbury, www.pillsbury.com
Pixar, www.pixar.com
Porsche, www.porsche.com
Price-Costco, www.pricecostco.com
Procter & Gamble, www.pg.com

Red Dog beer, www.reddog.com:443

Sam's Club, www.samsclub.com
San Jose Mercury, www.sjmercury.com
Science, www.sciencemag.org
Sears Roebuck and Company, www.sears.com
Silk Road, The Story of, http://ess1.ps.usi.edu/~oliver/silk.html
Smart Valley, www.svi.org
Smith Barney, www.smithbarney.com
Sony Music, www.sony.com
Spin magazine, www.enews.com/magazines/spin
Sri-Lanka, www.tbc.gov.bc.ca/cwgames/country/SriLanka/
    srilanka.html

Stanford Computer Industry Project,
    www-scip.stanford.edu/scip
Starbright Pediatric Network, www.starbright.org
Sun Microsystems, www.sun.com
Swiss Direct Democracy, www.vote.org/v/swiss2.htm

Tele-communications, Inc. (TCI), www.tci.com

U.S. Geological Survey, wwwneic.cr.usgs.gov
Unilever, www.tasteyoulove.com
Universal Studios, www.univstudios.com
University of Michigan Business School, www.bus.umich.edu
Upside magazine, www.upside.com

Visa International, www.VISA.com

Wal-Mart Stores, www.wal-mart.com
Wall Street Journal, www.wsj.com
Walt Disney Company, www.disney.com
Washington Post, www.washingtonpost.com
Washington State University,
    www.sci.wsu.edu/math/courses/on_line_courses.html
Wave Sport, http://hos.madboulder.com/~eprincen/WaveSport
Weblogic, www.weblogic.com
Wharton School, University of Pennsylvania,
    www.wharton.upenn.edu
Wired magazine, www.wired.com

Notes

Introduction

1. Alvin Toffler, *Future Shock* (New York: Random House, 1970), 371.
2. Edward Feigenbaum, Shirley Tessler, and Avron Barr, *Stanford Computer Industry Project Study* (Stanford University, Palo Alto, Calif., 1994).

Chapter 1

1. Michael Kammen, *Mystic Chords of Memory* (New York: Alfred A. Knopf, 1991), 246.
2. Jane L. Levere, Advertising Column, and John Markoff, "AT&T Plans to Offer Internet over $500 Wireless Phone," *New York Times*, July 12, 1996.
3. George Lipsitz, *Time Passages* (Minneapolis: University of Minnesota Press, 1990).
4. Scott McNealy is generally credited with the phrase "The network is the computer."
5. Molly Moore, "In Far Northwest India, Mountain Tribes Meet the World," *Washington Post*, December 26, 1992.
6. Vibha Chhabra, from unpublished article given to the author, 1997.
7. "The Satellite Biz Blasts Off," Special Report, *Business Week*, January 27, 1997.
8. Brian Beedham, "A Better Way to Vote," in *The Future Surveyed*, a special 150th anniversary supplement to *Economist*, September 11, 1993.
9. Yuri Radzievsky, "Untapped Markets, Ethnics in the U.S.," *Advertising Age*, June 21, 1993.

Chapter 2

1. "Americans Can't Get No Satisfaction," *Fortune*, December 11, 1995.
2. This example is taken from my essay "Real Time Marketing," *Harvard Business Review*, July–August 1995.
3. See "Fashion Relearns Its Darwin: Be Adaptable or Be Extinct," the second installment of a two-part article about the women's garment industry, *New York Times*, August 6, 1996.
4. Matt Nauman, "The Porsche Predicament," *San Jose Mercury News*, March 11, 1994.
5. "Fashion Relearns Its Darwin: Be Adaptable or Be Extinct," *New York Times*, August 6, 1996.
6. Ibid.
7. Natan Sharansky, *Fear No Evil* (New York: Random House, 1988).
8. *Trainspotting: A Screenplay* (New York: Miramax Books, 1996). Adapted by John Hodge from the novel of the same name by Irvine Walsh.
9. Patents Column, *New York Times*, June 17, 1996.
10. Dave Power, J. D. Power and Associates, October 18, 1996, interview with the author.
11. Nadine Gordimer, "My Century," *World Link*, May–June 1996.
12. Regis McKenna, "Marketing Is Everything," *Harvard Business Review*, January–February 1991.

Chapter 3

1. Nicholas Negraponte, *Being Digital* (New York: Alfred A. Knopf, 1995), 84.
2. David Berwick, director of the Mountain Dew brand, interview with the author, August 14, 1996.
3. Kenneth N. Gilpin, "The Kitchen Sink and More; A Franchiser Is Selling Homes and All the Trimmings," *New York Times*, August 9, 1996.
4. "P&G's Artzt: TV Advertising in Danger," Procter and Gamble CEO Edwin L. Artzt's address at the American Association of

Advertising Agencies conference, transcript, *Advertising Age*, May 23, 1994.

5. Anthony Smith, president of Magdalen College, Oxford, and a former director of the British Film Institute, writing in a special supplement to the *Economist*, September 11, 1993.

6. Saul Hansell, "The Ante Rises in East Asia," *New York Times*, July 14, 1996.

7. Witold Rybczynski, "Tomorrowland," *New Yorker*, July 22, 1996.

8. David W. Chen, "Amish Going Modern, Sort of, about Skating," *New York Times*, August 11, 1996.

9. David Denby, "Buried Alive," *New Yorker*, July 15, 1996.

Chapter 4

1. David Reibstein, *Marketing: Concepts, Strategies, and Decisions* (Englewood Cliffs, N.J.: Prentice-Hall, 1984), 279.

2. Alan Mitchell, "Brand Imagery Costs Pilloried," *Financial Times* (London), January 6, 1997.

3. Raju Naisetti, "Too Many Choices, P&G, Seeing Shoppers Were Being Confused, Overhauls Marketing," *Wall Street Journal*, January 15, 1997.

4. Ibid.

5. Ibid.

6. George Horn, "Where Are You, Captain Nemo?" *Manufacturing Systems*, June 1992, 44–45.

7. Keith Bradsher, "GM's Labor Costs on Parts Said to Be Higher Than Rivals," *New York Times*, June 25, 1996.

8. Dave Power, interview with author.

9. Theodore Roszak, "High Tech Fury," *San Jose Mercury News*, June 30, 1996.

10. Regis McKenna, "Marketing in an Age of Diversity," *Harvard Business Review*, September–October 1988, and "Marketing Is Everything," *Harvard Business Review*, January–February 1991 (reprints available through custserv@cchbspub.harvard.edu).

11. Peter Drucker, *The New Realities* (New York: Harper & Row, 1989).

Chapter 5

1. Anna Lee Saxenian, "The Origins and Dynamics of Production Networks in Silicon Valley," a working paper published by the Institute of Urban and Regional Development at the University of California at Berkeley, April 1990.
2. Ibid.
3. Ali Kutay, interview with author, September 1996.
4. Lee Sproull and Sara Kiesler, "Computers, Networks, and Work," *Scientific American*, September 1991.
5. Ibid.
6. Ali Kutay, interview with author.
7. Bill Gates in his "Technology" column, *PriceCostco Connection*, October 1996.
8. Barnaby J. Feder, "Kennametal Finds the Right Tools," *New York Times*, May 6, 1992.
9. David Upton and Andrew McAffee, "The Real Virtual Factory," *Harvard Business Review*, July–August 1996 (reprints available through custserv@cchbspub.harvard.edu).
10. Ibid.

Chapter 6

1. Freeman Dyson, *Infinite in All Directions* (New York: Harper & Row, 1985.)
2. Networking-oriented minicomputer manufactured by Hewlett-Packard rival Digital Equipment Corporation.
3. Joel Birnbaum, interview with the author, August 6, 1996.
4. "Guide to the New Economy," *Fortune*, June 27, 1994.
5. "Do Call Us: More Companies Install 1-800 Phone Lines," *Wall Street Journal*, April 24, 1994.
6. "A Nation of Browsers," *Economist*, September 7, 1996.
7. George Gilder, "Telecocosm Feasting on the Giant Peach," *Forbes ASAP*, August 26, 1996.
8. Notes on MacCready's speech taken by the author.
9. Jamshid Gharajedaghi, *Total Quality Review*, March/April 1994, 11–18. © MCB University Press, 1353–1603.

10. Michael E. Porter, *Competitive Advantage: Creating and Sustaining Superior Performance* (New York: Free Press, 1985).

Chapter 7

1. Barnaby J. Feder, "Highs and Lows Are Their Business," *New York Times*, October 22, 1996.
2. Dyson, *Infinite in All Directions*.
3. Stephan H. Haeckel and Richard L. Nolan, "Managing by Wire," *Harvard Business Review*, September–October 1993.
4. Allen R. Janger, *Management Outlook 1985* (New York: Conference Board, 1984).

Epilogue

(*Note*: Source of Robert Solow quote in the first epigraph in the chapter is Louis Uchitelle, "We're Leaner, Meaner and Going Nowhere Faster," *New York Times*, May 12, 1996.)

1. Eric Brynjolfsson, "The Productivity Paradox of Information Technology," *Communications of the ACM*, December 1993.
2. David Cay Johnston, "I.R.S. Admits Lag in Modernization; Urges Contract Plan," *New York Times*, January 31, 1997.
3. Thomas A. Bass, "The Future of Money," an interview with Walter Wriston, *Wired*, October 1996.
4. Warren E. Leary, "Ground Tests Loom for Ultimate Hot Rods, Supersonic Cars," *New York Times*, October 1, 1996.

Index

About the Author

REGIS MCKENNA is chairman of The McKenna Group, a management and marketing consulting firm specializing in the development and application of information and telecommunications technologies located in Palo Alto, California.

McKenna is active as an independent investor who has seeded over a dozen start-ups, including Weblogic (www.web logic.com), a database connectivity, java software company in San Francisco; Graham Technologies (www.graham.com), a video Internet network company; and Real Time Knowledge Systems (www.rtks.com), a developer of collaborative marketing tools that allow users to "learn and do" across intranets.

He was responsible for helping to launch some of the most important technological innovations of the past twenty-five years, including the first microprocessor (Intel Corporation), the first personal computer (Apple Computer), the first recombinant DNA genetically engineered product (Genentech, Inc.), and the first retail computer store (The Byte Shop). Other groundbreaking technology marketing efforts in which he participated include the first commercial laser for retail systems, the first computer local area network, the first electronic spreadsheet, the first operating system for personal computers, the first mini-supercomputers, and the first desktop publishing systems.

McKenna has worked with a number of entrepreneurial start-ups during their formative years, including America Online, Apple, Businessland, Compaq, Electronic Arts, Genentech, Intel, Linear Technology, Lotus, Microchip, Microsoft, National Semiconductor, Sequent, Silicon Graphics, Tandem, and 3COM. In the past decade, he has consulted on strategic marketing and business issues to many of the largest technology-based firms in the United States, Japan, and Europe. He is a venture partner with Kleiner Perkens Caufield & Byers (www.kpcb.com), one of the most successful venture capital firms in Silicon Valley.

He is a founding board member of Smart Valley (www.svi.org), a Silicon Valley project to create an information highway linking businesses, schools, governments, and homes; a member of the advisory board to Stanford's Graduate School of Business (www-gsb.stanford.edu); a trustee at Santa Clara University (http://scuish.scu.edu); and president of the board of trustees for The New Children's Shelter of Santa Clara County.

McKenna is the author of three other books—*The Regis Touch*, *Who's Afraid of Big Blue?*, and *Relationship Marketing*—and several articles. Currently, he lectures and conducts seminars on technology marketing and competitiveness issues throughout the United States, Europe, and Asia.

$$\text{Hrs.} \times \frac{\text{Min}}{\text{Hr}}$$